Readers will enjoy an exhilarating climb of Mt. Rainier with Pat Williams—and learn practical lessons for a more fulfilling life.

JACK RAMSAY, NBA AND COLLEGE BASKETBALL COACHING LEGEND

Pat Williams does it again. He is a powerful writer and his vivid description of life while climbing Mt. Rainier is breathtaking. Pat Williams's book is awesome, baby!

DICK VITALE, COLLEGE BASKETBALL TELEVISION ANALYST

Secrets from the Mountain is one of the best inspirational books I've ever read. His ten lessons for life are so convincing and so useful to everyone that I will share these frequently with our Gator football team.

STEVE SPURRIER, UNIVERSITY OF FLORIDA HEAD FOOTBALL COACH

Pat Williams has written another marvelous motivational and inspirational book. This time you will climb Mt. Rainier with him and your life will be deeply impacted by his exciting journey.

DR. JOHN C. MAXWELL, FOUNDER, THE INJOY GROUP

Pat Williams's book, *Secrets from the Mountain*, contains valuable lessons for anyone who is willing to risk and to grow. Pat has an excellent spiritual base from which he writes and this perspective makes his observations and principles even more valuable. I certainly recommend *Secrets from the Mountain* as outstanding reading.

TOM OSBORNE, FORMER HEAD FOOTBALL COACH, UNIVERSITY OF NEBRASKA

Pat Williams has been climbing mountains and winning victories most of his life. His newest book, *Secrets from the Mountain*, will push you to new heights in your own journey to the summit of your dreams.

DR. JERRY FALWELL, CHANCELLOR, LIBERTY UNIVERSITY, LYNCHBURG, VA.

Pat Williams clearly demonstrates that the key lessons to successful living are all around us if we would simply pay close attention. The lessons he learned from the slopes of Mt. Rainier will help elevate your life from the valley of despair and defeat to the precipice of victory and hope.

DR. TONY EVANS, PRESIDENT, THE URBAN ALTERNATIVE

Pat Williams's books always make for fun reading. This one is not only fun but the wonderful lessons he learned on Mt. Rainier will stick with you and bless you for a lifetime. Guaranteed.

DR. BILL BRIGHT, FOUNDER AND PRESIDENT, CAMPUS CRUSADE FOR CHRIST

Pat Williams, having thrown himself against the summit of Mount Rainier, lifts the window of his soul and becomes a teacher for his readers. His message of the mountain provides timely and vital life-changing wisdom worth deep reflection.

HOWARD G. HENDRICKS, DISTINGUISHED PROFESSOR AND CHAIRMAN, CENTER FOR CHRISTIAN LEADERSHIP, DALLAS THEOLOGICAL SEMINARY

Pat Williams's spirit of adventure is both inspiring and insightful. Mount Rainier is a great teacher and Pat has captured that reality beautifully in *Secrets from the Mountain*.

JIM LOEHR, MOTIVATIONAL SPEAKER AND AUTHOR

We've all faced fear and doubt. Pat Williams shares with us his experience and how to deal with both. Great reading because it is written in a way that we can all relate to.

DAN REEVES, HEAD COACH, ATLANTA HAWKS

It is not news that Pat Williams climbed a mountain. It will be news however when he doesn't!

DAN PATRICK, ESPN

An absolute inspiration! Pat Williams's story of courage and determination will convince people of all ages that with God, they too can climb *any* mountain.

RICH DEVOS, COFOUNDER OF THE AMWAY CORPORATION AND
CHAIRMAN OF THE ORLANDO MAGIC

In *Secrets from the Mountain*, Pat Williams has demonstrated that a discerning eye and a keen intellect can glean much wisdom from the experiences of life. He has shown us that we can ignore these lessons or we can allow them to help us realize the potential that God has placed in each of us.

BENJAMIN S. CARSON, SR., M.D., DIRECTOR OF PEDIATRIC NEUROSURGERY,
JOHNS HOPKINS

Nobody motivates me like Pat Williams. When I finished *Secrets from the Mountain*, I wanted to run a marathon. Then I realized this book was helping to prepare me for the ultimate—the race of life. If you're content to stay where you are, don't read this book!

DR. DAVID JEREMIAH, PRESIDENT, TURNING POINT

The life lessons that Pat Williams, author and climber, experienced on Mount Rainier reflect our thoughts over forty years of climbing and guiding. To read these lessons that we have only thought about has given us more reasons to climb and experience life. This is a must-read book for any climber of Mount Rainier or other "Everests of Life."

INGRID AND LOU WHITTAKER, WORLD CLASS MOUNTAIN CLIMBERS

We all must face mountains in our life. I truly believe Pat Williams's book provides practical answers to climbing these mountains more successfully.

DAN QUAYLE, FORMER VICE-PRESIDENT OF THE UNITED STATES

I could not have read Pat Williams's latest book at a more meaningful time. His thoughts and those of others within the book were exactly the same principles I was selling to a pro football organization on the way to their first Super Bowl win. Therefore, Pat added credibility to our approach. No matter how much one achieves, he needs constant revitalization, and Pat's book did that for me.

DICK VERMEIL, FORMER HEAD COACH, ST. LOUIS RAMS,
2000 SUPER BOWL CHAMPIONS

Pat Williams's book is filled with timeless inspiration of lessons to be learned for living. This is a book of truth and hope in making every moment count. *Secrets from the Mountain* is a metaphor for seeking the peak and having the courage to dream big and believe you can make it to the top! Start, then step, and never stop living, learning, and loving. A must read!

DEBBI FIELDS, MOTHER OF FIVE AND FOUNDER AND CHIEF COOKIE LOVER,
MRS. FIELDS COOKIES

It is no wonder that Pat Williams, one of our generation's most creative, imaginative, vibrant, dynamic, prolific authors, has generated yet another masterpiece, this one about the successful yet always dangerous and elusive journey to the top of the mountain. This fascinating read weaves the great struggles in life with the awesome forces of nature and the human spirit. Pat Williams is at his best here and that's no easy task since he's already been on top of the mountain for so long.

BILL WALTON, BASKETBALL HALL OF FAMER AND NBC BROADCASTER

Every time Pat Williams writes a book, he touches the heart. His latest work, *Secrets from the Mountain* is my new favorite. It will elevate your spirit and help change your life.

JACK KEMP, CODIRECTOR, EMPOWER AMERICA

Everyone has a mountain to climb, and reading the challenges Pat has faced will make yours easier to bear.

MARK VICTOR HANSEN, COCREATOR, #1 *NEW YORK TIMES* BEST-SELLING SERIES,
CHICKEN SOUP FOR THE SOUL

Pat Williams is amazing. He is always learning and cares about your goals and dreams. Read *Secrets from the Mountain!* It will make a real difference in your life.

KEN BLANCHARD, COAUTHOR OF *THE ONE MINUTE MANAGER* AND
LEADERSHIP BY THE BOOK

God uses real-life experiences to teach us greater life lessons. As he ascended Mount Rainier, Pat Williams gained spiritual insights that will inspire us all. *Secrets from the Mountain* gives us 10 practical lessons that will help us lift our sights to loftier horizons.

JAMES ROBISON, PRESIDENT, LIFE OUTREACH INTERNATIONAL, FT. WORTH, TEX.

Pat Williams is a man of great accomplishment. I expect you will learn from his life and this book things worth applying to your life.

CAL THOMAS, SYNDICATED COLUMNIST

Pat Williams has a unique way of taking the events of life and applying them to all of our lives. This story about climbing Mt. Rainier is his best work yet.

JACK CANFIELD, COAUTHOR, *CHICKEN SOUP FOR THE SOUL* SERIES

A marvelous book—lessons for everyone. I salute Pat Williams for sharing his life experiences. If our football players live by Pat's teachings, we will always be successful.

BILL WALSH, GENERAL MANAGER, SAN FRANCISCO 49ERS

Pat Williams, inspired by his encounter with ice-clad Mount Rainier, has taken the "mountain-as-metaphor" axiom to new heights with this valuable and highly readable guide to meeting life's challenges.

JIM WICKWIRE, MOUNTAIN CLIMBER AND AUTHOR

I am always interested to hear what Pat Williams has to say or write. That's why I'm excited about his latest book. Pat is constantly striving for more experiences and knowledge. My only question is, "Where in the world does he get the energy?" He'll probably tell you the strength does not come from this world, but from his dedication to his Christian faith.

BOBBY BOWDEN, HEAD FOOTBALL COACH, FLORIDA STATE UNIVERSITY

Secrets from the Mountain is Pat Williams's best book yet—this tops the list!

BOBBY COX, MANAGER, ATLANTA BRAVES

Finally, a book that vividly and inspiringly illustrates what "Carpe diem" really means to each of us: "Seize the day," and climb your mountains as they appear in the now. Pat Williams is the ultimate peak performer!

DR. DENIS WAITLEY, AUTHOR, *THE PSYCHOLOGY OF WINNING*

Pat Williams is one of the nation's greatest motivational speakers and writers. This new book will really help me as I tackle the mountains of my life. The same goes for you.

TERRY BRADSHAW, NFL HALL OF FAME QUARTERBACK

SECRETS

F·R·O·M T·H·E

MOUNTAIN

SECRETS

F·R·O·M T·H·E

MOUNTAIN

TEN LESSONS *for* SUCCESS IN LIFE

PAT WILLIAMS
WITH DAVID WIMBISH

Fleming H. Revell
A Division of Baker Book House Co
Grand Rapids, Michigan 49516

Published by Fleming H. Revell
a division of Baker Book House Company
P.O. Box 6287, Grand Rapids, MI 49516-6287

Printed in the United States of America

Library of Congress Cataloging-in-Publication Data

Williams, Pat, 1940–
    Secrets from the mountain : ten lessons for success in life / Pat Williams with David Wimbish.
      p.   cm.
    Includes bibliographical references (p.).
    ISBN 0-8007-1779-1
    1. Success—Religious aspects—Christianity. I. Wimbish, David.
II. Title.
BV4598.3.W55 2001
158.1—dc21   00-051787

The following permissions to reprint are acknowledged:

Excerpt from *Our Daily Bread* by Vernon C. Grounds © 2000 by RBC Ministries, Grand Rapids, Mich. Reprinted by permission

Excerpt from *Two for the Summit: My Daughter, the Mountains and Me* by Geoffrey Norman, NAL-Dutton, 1999. Used by permission.

For current information about all releases from Baker Book House, visit our web site:
http://www.bakerbooks.com

This book is dedicated, with much love, to my daughter Karyn. May this book serve as a guide to you as you begin climbing the mountains in your life.

▼

Contents

ACKNOWLEDGMENTS

IT IS WITH DEEP APPRECIATION that I acknowledge the support and guidance of the following people, without whom these secrets from the mountain could not have made it to the printed page:

Special thanks go to Bob Vander Weide, John Weisbrod, and Bill Boer of the RDV Sports family.

I have deep appreciation for my assistant Melinda Ethington—thank you so much for all you've done, and do!

Kudos to two other trusted associates: Leslie Boucher and Hank Martens.

Hearty thanks are also due to Bill Petersen, Mary Wenger, Mary Suggs, and Twila Bennett of Fleming H. Revell, and to my cohort in writing this book, David Wimbish. Thank you all for believing that I had something important to say and for providing the forum to say it.

Thank you to proofreader extraordinaire Ken Hussar. Great job, Ken!

And finally, special thanks and appreciation go to my wife, Ruth, my most valuable assistant in all phases of this book. I love you, Ruth!

O·N·E

"Pat, You Must Be Crazy!"

Impossibilities vanish when a man and his God confront a
mountain.

ROBERT SCHULLER

We live and learn, and big mountains are stern teachers.

BILL TILMAN, ENGLISH MOUNTAINEER

My FRIENDS WERE CONVINCED I was suffering from a midlife
crisis.

"Pat," one of them said, "why don't you just buy yourself a little red sports car?"

When I politely declined and told them my mind was made up,
I could see the bewilderment in their eyes. They clearly thought I
had lost my mind. And maybe I had . . . momentarily.

I really don't know what got into me, but for some reason, in
December of 1995, I decided that I was going to run in my first

long-distance race—a half-marathon through the streets of Orlando, Florida. I had no idea if I was going to be able to finish the 13.1 mile course, but I knew I was going to try.

I was in pretty good shape. I ran regularly and lifted weights every day. But I still didn't know if I could run 13.1 miles. Like most people in today's world, I'm used to hopping in the car, even if I'm just going to the corner store for a few groceries.

When the big day came, I'm sure I felt like Christopher Columbus when he was about to set sail on his historic voyage. I was afraid that I was going to fall off the edge of the world at any moment. I'd heard runners talk about hitting the wall—when your body gives out on you and you can't possibly take another step. I was wondering if I was going to embarrass myself and prove that all my well-meaning friends were right.

But it didn't turn out that way.

To my amazement, I finished that race. I didn't set any course records, that's for sure, but when I crossed the finish line, I felt absolutely wonderful. It was exhilarating. I was proud of what I had been able to accomplish, and that meant a great deal to me, because there wasn't much I was proud of at that point in my life. I was going through a divorce—feeling depressed, embarrassed, and, frankly, humiliated. My wife, Jill, who had been my partner for twenty-three years, was getting ready to file for divorce in a few weeks. I had always thought that Jill and I had a good marriage. We had even written books on how to keep a marriage strong and healthy . . . and now ours was over. I was going through a terrible time.

That half-marathon didn't make all my troubles go away, but it gave me a good feeling for the first time in many months.

After the race, almost as soon as I had showered and dressed, the thought hit me. *I wonder if I could run a full marathon.* I wasn't certain I could but I knew I was going to try.

The Disney Marathon in Orlando was less than a month away, so I immediately began preparations. On marathon day, I was one of thousands of men and women who showed up at Disney World at 6 A.M. on an unseasonably chilly morning. It was really something! Music blared. Spotlights sliced through the early morning darkness. And then we were off!

16

Once again, I didn't set any records. There were ten thousand runners in that race, and I'm sure I saw the backsides of about eight thousand of them. But I didn't care about speed. I just wanted to finish. And I did, in just a little over five hours. What's more, crossing that finish line was one of the most emotional moments of my life!

Remember how Dick Vermeil was crying after the St. Louis Rams won Super Bowl XXXIV? Well, as I neared the end of that course on that winter morning, I was crying so hard, I made Coach Vermeil at his most emotional moment look as cold and stone-faced as a cigar-store Indian.

Tears flooded down my face, tears of joy, tears of pride, tears of exhilaration. What an overwhelming feeling!

Something ignited in my soul that day, and I realized that all of us can do a whole lot more than we think we can. But we can't do it unless we try.

I went on to compete in a number of other marathons that year and—lo and behold—I finished them too! I even pulled some strings with my friends in the Boston Celtics organization and joined thirty-two thousand other runners for the historic one hundredth running of the Boston Marathon in April of 1996. I finished the course in five hours, nine minutes, and fifty-seven seconds.

Once again, tears were rolling down my cheeks as I passed the final checkpoint and headed down the home stretch. Strange, because I'm not known as someone who has to carry a handkerchief in his pocket because he cries all the time. I'm a man, after all . . . and a man who grew up in an era when males were simply not allowed to cry.

I was crying because God was doing something inside of me. I was learning that the old adage really is true: "There's nothing God and you together can't do." There was also a twinge of sorrow in those tears because of the realization of all the times in the past when I had limited myself, or when I didn't try something new because I was afraid I couldn't do it.

By the time I crossed the finish line in the Boston Marathon, all the Kenyan runners had showered, put their street clothes back on, and were on their airliner headed for home. But I came away with three more hours of memories than they did!

It was while I was showering after that marathon that a dangerous thought came to me: *What next?*

The following month newscasts all over the world were full of the tragic news that eight mountain climbers had been killed on Mount Everest—the worst catastrophe in the long history of Everest attempts. Veteran climber Jon Krakauer recounted that ill-fated climb in his book *Into Thin Air*, which is still on the *New York Times* bestseller list.

> ▲
>
> The one thing that will guarantee the successful conclusion of a doubtful undertaking is faith, in the beginning, that you can do it.
>
> WILLIAM JAMES
>
> ▼

Strange again, because you might think that news of a mountain-climbing disaster would serve to keep you as far away from mountains as you could possibly get. But it had the opposite effect on me. The moment I heard the news of that climb, I was obsessed. I kept thinking, *I wonder if I could climb a mountain.*

I knew absolutely nothing about mountain climbing, mountains being pretty scarce in Florida. (I think the highest peak in the state is just to the right of Fantasyland and has a bobsled rollercoaster running through it.)

The only mountain I could think of was Mount Rainier. I didn't even know where it was. I remembered that there had once been a baseball team in the Pacific Coast League called the Seattle Rainiers, so I figured the mountain must be somewhere in Washington State.

I checked around and found out that I was right. Mount Rainier is a semidormant volcano in the Cascades of west-central Washington State. I also discovered there is an organization that leads climbs up the mountain on a daily basis.

Mount Rainier is the tallest glacier peak in the forty-eight contiguous states, topping out at 14,410 feet. Although I didn't know it at the time, Rainier is also often used by climbers as preparation for an assault on Mount Everest. That's because even though Rainier is nearly 15,000 feet shorter than the world's tallest mountain, some of the terrain and conditions are very similar to what you would find on Everest. Had I known any of this, I might have approached this new adventure with a little less enthusiasm. Or I might have looked for a different (shorter) mountain to climb!

I am grateful that I didn't know what veteran climber Lou Whittaker has to say about Mount Rainier: "There's no better training ground for Everest than Mount Rainier. Climbers come here from all over the United States to train for big climbs. There are twenty-seven glaciers on Rainier, and the weather can drop to 50 below in the winter."

He goes on: "Geologists call Mount Rainier an arctic island in the middle of a temperate zone. The snow and ice of Rainier is a perfect place in which to prepare for the two or three months that climbers will spend in the lifeless blue and white environment of Everest. . . . Mount Rainier is a great equalizer. It doesn't matter if you're a blue-collar worker or the head of a big corporation. The mountain treats you the same. I really enjoy taking up corporate executives."

The more I looked into climbing the mountain, the more I thought it was perfect for an amateur like me. All I had to do was buy a few pieces of equipment, make the trip to Rainier, take the one-day training course, and the next day I'd be heading up the mountain. It seemed perfect, so I signed up.

As the date of my climb approached, I read everything I could find about mountain climbing. Finally, the appointed day arrived—and I boarded an airplane bound for Seattle.

▲

News Flash: Mountains can be dangerous!

▼

I got my first glimpse of the mountain from that airplane, and it was almost enough to make me want to turn back. We were about thirty minutes out of Seattle, when the pilot announced, "If you'll look out the left side of the airplane, you can get a breathtaking view of Mount Rainier."

He was right. The view certainly took my breath away! Rainier looked rugged, majestic, and scary! And what was all that white stuff? It couldn't be snow, since this was the end of August! But it was snow. Lots and lots of snow!

Well, maybe it didn't look quite so frightening if you were looking at it from the ground up! So I rented a car in Seattle and made the two-hour drive to the entrance of Mount Rainier National Park.

19

Understand, I'm about the farthest thing from an outdoorsman you'll ever meet. My idea of roughing it is bad service at the Holiday Inn. But there I was in Washington, starting training for my baptism of wind, ice, and nosebleed altitude.

> ▲
>
> Rainier is an amazing mountain, and not a small mountain. For almost forty years, I've been climbing in the Himalayas … and I've seen storms on Rainier as bad as storms in the Himalayas.
>
> SHERPA NAWANG GOMBU
>
> ▼

There were five of us in my group: a businessman from Ohio, another from Michigan, a husband-wife team from Wisconsin, and a guy from Orlando who wouldn't know a crevasse from a hole in the ground. Our instructor for the first day was an experienced climber by the name of Heather MacDonald. She took us by the scruff of the neck and whipped us into a team. She taught us how to traverse ice, how to use an ice ax to keep ourselves from falling off the mountain, how to rope ourselves together and work in unison—all the fundamentals of mountain climbing. The more she taught us, the more I began to think, *Hey, this mountain-climbing business could be dangerous!*

I never had a more fitful night in my life. I tried counting sheep so I could sleep, but they kept turning into mountain goats. I couldn't get my mind off what I was going to be facing the next day.

We were to report at 9 A.M. to get final instructions before beginning the ascent up the mountain. Overnight, Mount Rainier seemed to have grown by several thousand feet! Suddenly, it didn't look like an American mountain. It looked more like someone had moved it in from the Himalayas overnight!

Still, my body was racing with adrenaline. I couldn't wait to get started. At 9:30 our leader arrived and introduced himself. His name: George Dunn. He was a real mountain man—tall, leathery, and squint-eyed. He looked like Bill Walton at 6'3", but hopefully with good knees and feet. Just looking at him inspired confidence. George had us all introduce ourselves and he introduced us to his two assistants. Then he explained what we could expect as we began heading up the side of the mountain. At 10 o'clock we began our ascent.

The first part of the climb was easy, walking over familiar green grass and brown dirt trails. After an hour or so, we took a short break and then resumed walking around a large formation of rocks. As we came around them we were suddenly presented with a breathtakingly clear view of what lay ahead. The view caused my breath to stick in my throat. Just ahead of us, a blizzard—the worst kind of blizzard called a whiteout—was gathering in our path.

As we continued our climb, snow began to fall. Lightly at first. Then harder and harder. For the next four hours we walked right into the teeth of that blizzard. Soon snow was falling so fast and furiously that I was unable to see my hand in front of my face. There were moments when I was on the verge of panic. I thought that my friends were right. *I must have been crazy to get myself into this. I moved from Philadelphia to Florida to get away from snow! What in the world am I doing here?*

▲

The big question: What am I doing here?

▼

At around 3:30 in the afternoon we finally reached a place they called Camp Muir, which was really nothing more than a wooden hut. But as far as I was concerned, it was the Mount Rainier Ritz Carlton. We were 10,000 feet above sea level, a little over 4,000 feet from the summit, and that is where we would make camp. There were bare bunks in the cabin so we could spread out our sleeping bags, but there was no plumbing, electricity, or in-room HBO.

"I'll get you up around midnight to resume the climb," George told us. "So get thawed out and grab as much rest as you can."

I spread out my sleeping bag and settled in for a few hours of sleep. It was there on that bunk, 10,000 feet up the side of a mountain, that I had a lengthy conversation with God, although I have to admit it was pretty one-sided. *What am I doing here, Lord?* I asked him. *This is my vacation! Couldn't you have told me to pick something easier—like joining the Marines?*

I didn't actually hear his reply, but I felt it: "Pat, I've got some lessons to teach you on this mountain, so keep your eyes and ears open." I also remembered what it says in the Bible: "Go out and stand on the mountain in the presence of the LORD, for the LORD is about to pass by" (1 Kings 19:11).

Eventually, I drifted off to sleep. But I didn't sleep for long. A little after midnight, I was awakened by the sound of boot steps on a rough wooden floor.

"Time to get up," someone shouted.

It was George Dunn. "It's a beautiful night out," he said. "Just right for climbing. The storm has stopped and you've got an hour to get ready. So get your crampons on, and let's hit the mountain!"

I crawled out of my sleeping bag and began getting ready for the climb. I put on my crampons—metal spikes that attach to your boots so you can dig into the ice when you walk. I grabbed a bite to eat and then topped off my ensemble with a helmet that had a miner's light on it—an absolute necessity for climbing mountains in the dark. By about 1:30 in the morning, our little team was all roped together and heading up the mountain.

Even though I was in marathon shape, I have never been physically pulverized by anything like I was by Mount Rainier. It had stopped snowing and the moon was illuminating the mountain, but the wind was still whipping all around us, and right through our heavy coats. We plowed ahead through snowdrifts that were above our knees.

By 4 A.M. we had made our way another 1,000 feet toward the summit. Every muscle in my body was screaming for rest, so I was more than ready when our guides told us it was time for a break.

We had reached a place called "Disappointment Cleaver." They didn't tell us why it had that name, and I wasn't sure I wanted to know. As I looked back down at the trail we had ascended, I realized that a step or two in the wrong direction at just about any moment could have sent me plummeting to a not-so-painless and very cold death. Maybe I should have stuck to marathons.

After about twenty minutes of conferring among themselves, our guides told me and two other members of my group that we were not going to be allowed to go the rest of the way to the top. They were going to proceed with the husband-wife team from Wisconsin, who were experienced climbers. But for the rest of us, it was time to turn back. We still had 3,000 feet to go before reaching the summit, but our lives were more important than making it all the way to the top. We'd have to come back and try it another time.

They got no argument from me.

I was surprised to discover that it was harder going back down than it had been climbing the mountain in the first place. But by the time I got back to camp at day's end, this book was beginning to take shape in my mind. On the flight back to Orlando the next morning, I began writing. I wrote fast and furiously, filling an entire notebook with thoughts about the lessons I had learned on the mountain.

Five years later, looking back on my Mount Rainier adventure, I have no doubt that God called me to that mountain because he had a special purpose in mind. That purpose was the writing of this book.

Just as Moses came down from the mountain with the Ten Commandments, I came down from Rainier with the Ten Life Lessons contained in these pages. Am I trying to compare myself with Moses or the words contained in these pages with the Ten Commandments? Of course not. What I am saying is that, like Moses, I was drawn to that mountain in a supernatural way. God wanted me to use what I learned there to make a better life for myself. And I believe he also wanted me to share those lessons with you, so you can do the same.

Not a day goes by that I do not think about Mount Rainier and the lessons I learned there. That mountain is a part of my life. Perhaps someday I will be able to return, and this time I will make it all the way to the top.

In Isaiah 49:11 God says, "And I will make all my mountains a way" (KJV). This verse tells me several important things about mountains:

▲ Every mountain you attempt to climb is God's mountain. He owns it, and any place you set your foot you are on his property and in his presence.

▲ You may see the mountain that stands before you as an obstacle, as a barrier to your goal, but in God's hands, it can become a "way" through which you grow and advance.

▲ Every mountain in your life, whatever it may be, is potentially a "way" for you to grow.

23

In this book, I will explore the Ten Life Lessons I learned on Mount Rainier with stories from that adventure and with application to all areas of your life—spiritual life, family life, business life, church life, and recreational life.

Are You Ready to Climb Your Mountains?

You may not want to go off and try to climb a mountain as I did. But the truth is that life is full of mountains, and we must climb them on an almost daily basis. My purpose in writing this book is to help you scale the mountains that confront you, no matter what those mountains may be, no matter how formidable they may appear. You *can* scale them. You *can* stand triumphantly on the summit.

I learned these lessons as I ascended the mountain, but I have listed them David Letterman–style, in descending order, from number ten to number one. Are you ready? Get your crampons on, and let's get started!

Life Lesson Number Ten: Live Large

If you ain't got a hole in the ice, you can't catch any perch.

STEPHEN KING

If we did all the things we are capable of doing, we would literally astound ourselves.

THOMAS EDISON

WHEN I DECIDED I WANTED TO RUN in a marathon, some of my friends were astounded. Some of them reminded me—and not always in very nice terms—that I wasn't as young as I used to be.

I knew what they were thinking. Marathons are meant for twenty-somethings in perfect physical shape—not for guys like me who are on the downhill side of fifty.

When I finished my first marathon in reasonably good shape, I could see the relief in their eyes. The attitude was, Okay, you proved you could do it. Now, thank goodness, maybe you've got that foolishness out of your system. From now on, just stay in your office, sitting behind your desk, pushing papers like you're supposed to.

You should have seen their faces when I told them I was going to climb Mount Rainier!

Don't get me wrong. Many friends and family members supported me all the way. They thought it was great that I was willing to push myself to the limit—to risk failure in the pursuit of a goal that was important to me. Besides, my greatest obstacle wasn't the negative attitude of friends and relatives. It was, instead, the voice of doubt within me. Almost from the day I decided to make the climb, a war raged inside of me. *Are you sure you really want to do this? What if you make a fool of yourself? What if something happens up on that mountain and you have to come back to Orlando and listen to everyone say, "I told you so"?*

I never paid a whole lot of attention to those negative voices, but they were always there until the very moment I boarded a Delta Airlines jet for Seattle. Certainly, I could have come home with my tail between my legs and spent the next several weeks listening to friends say, "I told you so." But even then, I would have had the satisfaction of knowing I had tried. And that's the first lesson I learned on Mount Rainier:

Whatever you want in life won't come to pass by your sitting around and waiting for it to happen. You've got to take steps to make it happen.

In 1985 adventurer Michael McGuire hiked across the Polar ice cap. When asked why he did it, McGuire replied, "I like to collect experiences the way other people like to collect coins and stamps."

Richard Pulliam is another man who seeks to live life to the fullest. Chances are you've never heard of him, but he's been a tremendous source of inspiration to me. Some people take life as it comes. Not Richard. He runs out and meets every experience head-on. He devours every single moment of every single day.

Two days before I flew to Seattle, I was asked to give a speech at a huge Amway convention in Memphis. That convention hall was absolutely rocking with enthusiasm and excitement, as Amway conventions always are. I couldn't help but feel pumped up after an experience like that. Talk about being high on life!

The day after I returned to Orlando from Mount Rainier, Pulliam telephoned me at my office. He told me how much he had enjoyed my speech, and then threw in the stunner. "I had a stroke eleven days ago," he said.

Before I could respond, he chuckled and went on. "But I told myself, *Nothing's going to keep me from that convention*. I'm sure glad I didn't let a little thing like a stroke stop me, because the rally was a tremendous boost. Thanks again for your message, Pat. You really inspired me."

Here was a man who, according to his doctors, should have been spending his days in bed. But he was determined that if there was any way he could be at that Amway convention, he was going to be there. *And he was telling me that I had inspired him!* I tried to tell him he had that backwards, but he wouldn't hear of it.

"Remember, Pat," he said, as he concluded our conversation, "live large!" *Live large!* I will never forget those two powerful words from a man who most definitely practices what he preaches. Anyone can "live large" by following these seven principles learned on the slopes of Mount Rainier:

1. It's okay to fail.
2. Don't be afraid to start (and starting is often the hardest part).
3. Dare to dream big.
4. Don't be afraid to try something new.
5. Take things one step at a time.
6. Keep moving forward.
7. The only thing that can stop you is you.

Let's take a closer look at each of these principles.

1. It's Okay to Fail

When I began to fear that I would fall flat on my face (and possibly with disastrous results) on Mount Rainier, I responded to those doubts by reminding myself that it is okay to risk failure. I knew that I would have a much easier time living with failure than with knowing I had never tried at all. I've heard it said that the risks we regret most in life are the risks we never take. I know that's true.

It's not only okay to take risks. It's vital. Here's something else important I want you to know: If I could do it, you can too!

▲

You can only become a winner if you are willing to walk over the edge.

RONALD E. MCNAIR,
BUSINESS EXECUTIVE

▼

Listen to these words of wisdom from Mark Twain: "Twenty years from now you will be more disappointed by the things you didn't do than by the ones you did. So throw off the bowlines, sail away from the safe harbor. Catch the trade winds in your sails. Explore. Dream." Here was a man who knew how to take risks—to live large.

Let me tell you about two other people who know about the importance of taking risks. The first is a young man by the name of Troyal. He was a pretty good athlete in high school and won a track scholarship to Oklahoma State University. He also excelled in baseball and thought about pursuing a professional career.

He was doing okay but he wasn't happy. Then one day he asked himself an important question: *If God came to earth with a box containing the reason for my life inside of it, what words would I most like to find in that box?*

The answer came immediately. *The music!*

He could play the guitar. Some said he had a pleasant voice. And he'd written some songs that he felt were surefire hits—if only he could get somebody to listen to them. And so, armed with that guitar, his great set of songs, and the willingness to take a risk to chase his dream, he set out for Nashville.

And do you know what happened? Absolutely nothing.

In Music City he was just one of thousands of would-be country music stars. So he gave up—temporarily—and went back to college. But he kept a tight grip on his dream, and two years later he decided to give the music business another try.

He and his wife, Sandy, went back to Nashville and took nine-to-five jobs. When Troyal wasn't busy making a living, he made the rounds of music publishers. The second time around was not turning out to be the charm. Nobody had been interested before. Nobody was interested now.

Then he heard about an "audition night" at a place called The Bluebird Café. He showed up, guitar in hand, and waited for his turn in the spotlight. Troyal wowed the audience that night. More important for him, he impressed a Columbia Records talent scout who caught his act. He was signed to a recording contract on the spot.

You say you've never heard of a country singer named Troyal? Sure you have. Only he goes by his middle name: Garth. And Troyal Garth Brooks has become the best-selling country artist of all time, selling more records than stars like Michael Jackson and Madonna.

The second person I want to tell you about is a young man named Erik Weihenmayer. Erik has been blind since the age of thirteen. Erik was determined not to be held back by a "little thing" like not being able to see. He joined his high school wrestling team and so impressed his teammates that they voted him cocaptain. He made it all the way to the state finals in his weight class, finishing second.

Next up, he decided to try his hand at rock climbing. Can you imagine what his friends must have said to him? "Rock climbing? Are you crazy? What if you fall? You could kill yourself."

Weihenmayer had an answer for them. "Blindness won't keep me from having fun." And it didn't.

He was very good at rock climbing and soon went on to bigger (some would say more dangerous) things. In 1995 he flew to Alaska and climbed Mount McKinley, North America's tallest mountain. The following year he became the first blind person ever to climb Yosemite's famous El Capitan, with granite walls rising straight into the sky for over 3,000 feet.

Today Weihenmayer teaches at a private school and says his blindness is "just a nuisance."

2. Don't Be Afraid to Start

I have a good friend who told me this story. "Over the years, I've written a number of books, and I always enjoy helping people make the most of their God-given potential. But writing a book isn't always as easy as it may appear. I'll never forget the first time I sat down and prepared to put my thoughts on paper. When I had been asked about writing the book, I had said, 'Sure, no problem.' I was excited. Then I sat down at my typewriter and started. Well, the truth is that I didn't start. What I did was stare at that blank paper—for what must have been hours. I was tortured by the questions running through my mind. *Where should I begin? What if I say the wrong thing? What if my words don't come out the way I want them to?* My mind raced on and on, while my hands rested idly on the keys.

▲

All glory comes from daring to begin.

EUGENE E. WARE, AUTHOR

▼

"Then I remembered some things I knew about the importance of taking risks. It didn't really matter if I got things right the first time. I could always go back and fix them later. I knew that taking risks is a part of any worthwhile endeavor, and that includes writing a book. I had to dare to begin. I took a deep breath and began to type.

"The first sentence wasn't so hard. The first paragraph was easier. The first page, easier still. Before long, the entire book was finished. I even met the publisher's deadline, and the response I got let me know that many people benefited from what I had to say.

"I took the risk, and I've been writing books ever since."

In 1997 I ran in the Chicago Marathon. For the last mile or so I was behind a woman wearing a black running shirt. On the back of that shirt, she had written these words in gold ink: "The miracle isn't that I finished. The miracle is that I had the courage to start." How true!

The poet and author Maya Angelou is a professor at my alma mater, Wake Forest University. She once wrote, "Some of us are timid. We think we have something to lose, so we don't try for the next hill."

I love this poem by Edgar A. Guest:

> Somebody said that it couldn't be done,
> But he with a chuckle replied
> That "maybe it couldn't" but he would be one
> Who wouldn't say no till he'd tried.
> So he buckled right in with the trace of a grin
> On his face. If he worried he hid it.
> He started to sing as he tackled the thing
> That couldn't be done, and he did it.
>
> USED BY PERMISSION

Some say that anything worth doing is worth doing well, and that's true. But I also believe that anything worth doing is worth starting! So whatever it is you want to do, don't be afraid to start. Do it now!

▲

3. Dare to Dream Big

The only death you die is the death you die everyday by not living. Dream big and dare to fail.

NORMAN VAUGHAN, AUTHOR

▼

When you were a child and people asked you what you wanted to be when you grew up, what did you say? Most of us saw ourselves becoming heroic figures of one kind or another: astronauts, presidents, superstar athletes, movie stars, or bold, daring adventurers, doing things like climbing the world's tallest mountains.

There's hardly a child alive who doesn't know how to dream—and dream big. But as we grow older, we often leave all of our dreams behind. Instead of replacing childhood dreams with adult dreams, we simply forget how to dream altogether. Too often we are willing to settle for boring, complacent lives. We not only forget how to dream, we become afraid to dream.

Author-theologian Elton Trueblood described it this way: "The chief tragedy in most lives is not dying, but making small what clearly could be made large. People all too frequently fill their minds with trifling matters, neglect opportunities, pursue insignificant purposes, and please themselves with things of little importance or merit. In man's small and uncaring ways, many people

31

find themselves doing things of minimal consequence. Many people do not live big lives—they live little ones."

How can we learn how to dream again? First, it involves asking ourselves what we'd really like to do if we could do anything we wanted to do. I'm afraid that most of us have become so stressed-out that we don't even know what we really want out of life. We don't let ourselves think about it, because we're too busy trying to make a living, providing for our children, and doing what we can to make other people happy.

So why not take some time right now to think about it? Get out a pen and notebook and make a list of the things you'd like to do with your life if everything were possible to you. And then decide what concrete steps you can take to make those dreams come true. The time to go for it is now!

I believe there are two main reasons why people stop dreaming big dreams:

The first reason we stop dreaming is because other people belittle our dreams.

I know all about this one. Remember that my decision to climb Mount Rainier wasn't met with resounding applause by everyone I knew. But on the other hand, there has never been a big dream anywhere at any time that wasn't called stupid by somebody. Some examples?

When Christopher Columbus proclaimed his intention to reach India by sailing west from Europe, instead of east, some members of the intelligentsia shook their heads sadly. They were worried about the fate that was going to befall the poor deluded fellow when he sailed right off the edge of the earth and into oblivion.

When Wilbur and Orville Wright were working on the invention called an "aeroplane," observers scoffed and remarked that if God had wanted human beings to fly, he would have given us feathers.

When Henry Ford, Louis Chevrolet, and others were perfecting the "horseless carriage" at the turn of the century, it was widely believed that human beings could never survive travel at speeds in excess of 20 miles an hour.

A motion picture executive of the 1920s said that "talkies" would never catch on because, after all, "who wants to hear actors talk?"

I could go on and on, but you get the picture. No wonder Albert Einstein said, "If, at first, the idea is not absurd, there is no hope for it." Clearly, the future belongs to those who see the possibilities before they become obvious.

Did you set aside your dreams because someone said they were silly or stupid? You can see from the examples given above that those dreamers who have been willing to press on ahead, regardless of what others were saying about them, are the ones who have changed our world.

So what if someone else thinks your dreams are dumb? What do they know? God hasn't called you to do what other people expect of you. He has called you to do something that is between you and him alone. I like what writer Cynthia Heimel says about this: "When in doubt, make a fool of yourself. There is a microscopically thin line between being brilliantly creative and acting like the most gigantic idiot on earth. So, what the heck? Leap!" Giovanni, a magician friend in Orlando, constantly reminds me: "If you're not living on the edge, you're taking up too much space."

The second reason we stop dreaming is because we let fear get in the way.

And this leads to a very important question. Namely, how can you overcome fear?

There's only one way I know of to do this, and that is to stare your fear in the face and keep moving in the direction of your dream—no matter how much your heart may be pounding, your knees shaking, or your brain telling you to turn back.

Was I ever afraid during my journey up the slopes of Mount Rainier? You bet I was! I was afraid from the moment I made up my mind that I was going to take the trip to Washington. I was afraid when I saw the mountain out of my airplane window. I was afraid when I saw the mountain for the first time from the ground up. And I was really afraid when the blizzard struck as we were making our way up the mountain on the first day.

Being afraid doesn't necessarily mean you're a coward. It may just mean that you've got the good sense to recognize that the road ahead may be difficult or dangerous. It is not cowardly to be afraid. The coward is the man who lets his fear get the best of him and runs away from any danger or challenge. The brave man is the one who persists, not because he has no fear, but in spite of his fear.

I spoke recently at a banquet in Sioux Falls, South Dakota. My host was a medical doctor who has one son who graduated from the United States Naval Academy and another son who graduated from the United States Air Force Academy. He told me: "The service academies teach their young people that courage is not the absence of fear, but the ability to control fear. They want pilots to fear and respect the fighter jets so they'll be very careful with them. They don't want to lose a pilot, but they also do not want to lose a $15 million plane."

Mountaineer Alan Hobson writes in his book *From Everest to Enlightenment*, "There are three steps to learning how to manage our fears. The first is to acknowledge that we are afraid. The second is to focus on the known, and the third is to take action. Most of us get stuck on step two. We focus on the unknown, not the known."

Hardly a day goes by that the Internet doesn't offer a fascinating mountain-climbing story. And these days they often find their way to my desk. One of Alan Hobson's stories graphically addresses this issue of fear: "Fear of the unknown is something we regularly face on Everest. On the southern approach to the mountain, we have to climb through the deadly Khumbu Icefall. This is a frozen river of ice that tumbles 2,000 feet over a rock ledge and in the process splits into ice blocks the size of hotels. The whole malignant mess is in constant motion. It moves a frightening one meter (3.28 feet) a day. On any other mountain, you would never dream of even going near such a feature, but on the southern side of Everest, in Nepal, you must climb through it if you hope to reach the summit.

"The Icefall is riddled with thousands of crevasses, some as much as fifteen stories deep. The only way to get over them is to walk across aluminum ladders temporarily bridged across them. The only problem is, you *have* to look down to see where you're placing your feet.

34

"One morning, as I gingerly made my way across a ladder, it began to bow, swaying up and down and creaking under my weight. A frigid gust of wind buffeted me from one side. To prevent myself from pitching sideways into the crevasse, I squeezed the safety lines like they were life itself.

"'You CAN survive, Alan,' I tried to reassure myself. 'You WILL.'

"When I got safely to the other side, I breathed a huge sigh of relief. Suddenly, I had a moment of dramatic realization. In facing fear, we have a choice of where we look—as far as the rungs of the ladder, or way . . . down into that terrifyingly deep hole beyond.

"We focus on all the terrible things that might befall us . . . or we can direct our energies to the small steps that can take us from where we are now to where we want to go. If we focus on our fears, we will end up in the crevasse. This is guaranteed. It is a law of nature.

"So, we must focus on our feet. That choice is 100 percent within our control. I know that because as time went on, I got better at crossing those terrifying ladders and I learned one of the ultimate truths of life . . .

" . . . on the other side of fear is freedom."

It's not often you can find wise words to live by in an advertisement. But this one from Nike has some wonderful advice for anyone who wants to live large:

> Too often, we are scared. Scared of what we might not be able to do. Scared of what people might think if we tried. We let our fears stand in the way of our hopes. We say "no," when we want to say "yes." We sit quietly when we want to scream, and we shout with the others when we should keep our mouths shut.
>
> Why? After all, we do only go around once. There's really no time to be afraid.
>
> So stop.
>
> Try something you've never tried. Risk it. Enter a triathlon. Write a letter to the editor. Demand a raise. Throw away your television. Bicycle across the USA. Try bobsledding. Try anything. Travel to a country where you don't speak the language. Patent something. Take the LSAT, just to see what you'd get. Call her. You have nothing to lose and everything, everything, everything to gain.

I have heard that there was a Persian general during World War II who allowed condemned prisoners to choose their fate. They could choose to be executed with the sword or they could decide to walk through a "big, black door." No one ever chose the door, preferring the horror of what they did know to the fear of what they did not know.

Toward the end of the war, someone asked the general what lay beyond the mysterious door. His answer: "Freedom." He said, "But people are afraid of that which is undefined and less certain. Behind the door is freedom, but few men are brave enough to take it."

▲

Unless you try to do something beyond what you have already mastered, you will never grow.

ANONYMOUS

▼

What are you afraid of? Dying in an airplane crash? Did you know that you have a greater chance of being killed by a kick from a donkey than you do of perishing in a plane crash? Are you afraid of riding on the train? You are more likely to be killed participating in a sport of some kind.

The truth is that if we could get outside of ourselves and view our fears from a new perspective, we'd see how comical they often are. Like the man who said, "I want to die peacefully in my sleep like my grandfather, not screaming and yelling like the passengers in his car."

I learned on the mountain that I cannot waste my time worrying about things that will most likely never come to pass. I am called to dream big, and to act on those dreams!

4. Dare to Try Something New

Another marathon: this time the Marine Corps Marathon in Washington. I was standing next to a woman from Baltimore as we awaited the sound of the starter's gun. On her shirt was the message, "When was the last time you did something for the first time?" For the next five hours, as I made my way through the streets of the capital, I kept reading those powerful words. It is so easy to dig ourselves into a rut of dull, boring sameness that can choke the life right out of us.

At that same race, I met an eighty-two-year-old woman from College Park, Maryland, who told me she was running in her eighth marathon. She had entered her first one ten years earlier. Can you imagine being seventy-two years old and deciding that you're going to run in a 26.2-mile race for the very first time in your life? But that's exactly what she did and, in the process, she found something that gave her joy and a sense of purpose.

It's never too late to try something new, to take a step in the direction of mystery and adventure. Or, as George Eliot put it: "It is never too late to be what you might have been."

Grandma Moses was seventy-six years old when arthritis in her fingers caused her to give up doing needlepoint, which she loved. She decided to try something new—painting. She quickly took the art world by storm, becoming one of the most respected artists of her time. Art collectors all over the world paid top dollar for her landscapes, and she continued with her newfound career— and success—well past her one-hundredth birthday.

There is no reason at all for you to stay in that rut, even if it is getting comfortable in there!

The other day, I ran into an old friend of mine and asked him how things were going. He shrugged and said, "Same ol' same ol'." I'm sure you've heard that same expression dozens of times. But, you know, anyone who keeps on doing things the same old way is going to get the same old results. If you did something yesterday and you didn't like the result you got, then why on earth would you do the very same thing again today? And tomorrow?

Am I saying that if you don't like your job, you should quit right now and hope something better comes along? Of course not. But I believe (as the Bible says in Psalm 37:4) that God wants to give you the desires of your heart. In other words, he wants you to have a life that brings you joy and satisfaction, not one that is causing what Thoreau called "quiet desperation." But my own experience tells me that he's not going to drop that life out of the sky and into your lap. He wants you to do what you can to move in the direction of your dreams, but he is willing to meet you more than halfway.

Abraham Lincoln said, "Towering genius disdains a beaten path. It seeks regions hitherto unexplored." I believe that all human beings, not just those who are blessed with "towering genius," yearn for "regions hitherto unexplored." Arctic explorer Fridtjof Nansen put it this way: "We all have a land of Beyond to seek in life. Our part is to find the trail that leads to it. . . . The call comes to us and we have to go. Rooted deep in the nature of every one of us is the spirit of adventure, vibrating under all our actions, making life deeper, higher and nobler."

In my own life, I strive to follow the example of renowned mountaineer Sir Edmund Hillary, who said, "All of my life, I've been afraid of having nothing to do, having no challenges to meet; being bored. Life has been a battle against boredom, but I've been quite good at thinking up adventures and carrying them out."

Believe me, no one is bored when he's risking his life to conquer a mountain, and all of us have mountains to climb.

Just as I was completing this book, I read *Two for the Summit* by Geoffrey Norman. I was fascinated with his observations on risk taking:

> The undeniable truth is that risk lies at the heart of the appeal of mountain climbing. There may be other reasons to climb mountains, but they are fairly tepid by comparison. It is risk that makes climbing so ineffably seductive. Trying to imagine climbing without risk is like trying to imagine seduction without sex.
>
> Taking risks and surviving is, quite simply, exhilarating. The sensation of danger is undeniably alluring and explains why amusement parks stay in business, selling tickets to the roller-coaster ride. You come away with a glow, happy to be alive. The greater, more genuine, and sustained the risk, the more profound the sensation. There are simulated risks, cheap thrills, like rides on the roller coaster, which you can buy for a couple of bucks and, then, there is genuine risk.
>
> There is a vast and essential difference between climbing and, say, bungee jumping. When you jump with a "reputable" outfit (if that word applies) you will scare the b——s out of yourself, but there is really no chance that you will be killed or injured. All the dangerous variables have been accounted for and are under the control of others. You are merely a paying passenger, along for the ride. Destination nowhere. The point of this trip is a simple adrenaline rush, pure sensation which you will have forgotten in an hour.
>
> When you climb, on the other hand, you take genuine risks and you manage them. You are hoping to get right up next to the edge of your ability and to dance there, in control, but just barely. You

not only feel the pump of danger but also a warm feeling of pride in having survived not merely by luck (which some people feel every time a passenger jet's wheels touch ground) or through grace, but from some combination of your own cool and skill. This, anyway, is the ideal. And it probably accounts for a lot of climbing's appeal. Somewhere in my random and undisciplined reading about climbing, I came across a line to the effect that climbing and bullfighting were the only true sports. Pretty thick and arch (which makes me think it might be Hemingway) but it holds a nugget.

Still, while all climbing is—in the locutions of the legal releases you sign—inherently risky, it is not suicidal or, probably, even as dangerous in an actuarial sense as some jobs. Coal mining or tree felling, for instance. And you don't see young college-educated people seeking out thrilling experiences in the West Virginia mines or the Oregon logging woods. There are no apparel companies turning out stuff with the coal miner or lumberjack look.

Which is to say, there is more to climbing than the possibility of a fall, frostbite, avalanche, and the other risks you take in the mountains.

USED BY PERMISSION

▲

You don't climb Everest by . . . just walking up the mountain. You first establish a base camp at 18,000 feet. . . . You then establish Camp One, at 20,000 feet . . . and then you start moving toward Camp Two, and so on. Finally, you get your fourth camp into place 3,000 feet below the summit, and it's from there that you launch the summit bid.

JOHN AMATT, MOUNTAIN CLIMBER

▼

5. Take Things One Step at a Time

Another thing I learned on Mount Rainier is that you can't make it to the top of a mountain in one giant step. Yes, you can move quickly at times. But there are other times when you have to move deliberately, picking your way ever so slowly and ever so carefully toward the summit.

Stacy Allison was the first American woman to reach the top of Mount Everest, accomplishing that feat in 1988. She was a college student at Oregon State University when she got her first taste of climbing—rappelling down a 50-foot fir tree. From that moment, she was hooked on climbing.

She went from trees to rock climbing. And then, in January of 1978, she undertook her first mountain-climbing adventure, on Rainier's sister peak, Mount Washington. The last 300 feet of that difficult climb took three hours to complete. That's less than 2 feet every minute! Talk about taking things one step at a time!

Stacy remembers that she was terribly cold, hungry, and exhausted. At the end of the climb, she was totally spent. But she was also elated and couldn't wait for her next climb.

Again going step-by-step, she worked her way toward the ultimate goal of all mountain climbers: Everest. She reached the top of the world at 10:30 A.M. on September 29, 1988. Looking back on that climb, she says, "Life is a constant maze of problems and puzzles. But . . . the key question is, how do you respond? What does your solution say about your life?"

Stacy is living proof that just about any goal you can set for yourself is attainable, if you are willing to take the necessary steps to reach it.

Chuck Harrelson shared with me his experience of climbing Mount Rainier. He said, "Having never attempted anything remotely close to this, I decided that this would be an opportunity to achieve something few people had and prove something to myself. The whole process of training for nearly a year and then climbing the mountain deepened my faith in God and in myself.

"Phil Erschler, our lead guide, spoke to our team right before we left. To paraphrase, Phil told us, 'Across the parking lot is the glacier room and our goal is to meet there in thirty-six hours to celebrate. But first we have to go on a little walk and take a roundabout way of getting there. When you leave this building, you can take a look up at the top of Mount Rainier, if you can see it, but after that it is best to not look at it for awhile. You see, the mountain is so high you can convince yourself that you'll never make it before you even get started. And when you're really tired, when you look up and see how far you have to go, you'll think there is no way you can make it.

"'So my advice to each of you is to see your goal at the beginning and then start walking. It's the only way to get there. Each time you think you can't go, just tell yourself that all you have to do is take *one more step*. As long as you can make yourself take one more step, you'll make it to the top and back again.'

"I can tell you that I thought about quitting a thousand times but I kept telling myself, *Just take one more step*. What a great lesson about how to achieve a goal! When I decided two and a half years ago to leave a comfortable career in medical sales to start my own company, I thought about that often. I still think about it today, and it still applies."

Candice Carpenter is an accomplished mountain climber and chief executive officer of Fast Company. She says, "It doesn't matter whether you are financing a new company, launching a brand on-line, raising a daughter or scaling a mountain . . . the process requires some specific steps."

Her advice, "First, imagine what you want to see in the world . . . something that doesn't exist; then take out a blank sheet of paper and design it. It could be a company, a product, a garden . . . anything." She adds, "If you aren't afraid of the hard times, obstacles become utterly unimportant." Slow and steady, step-by-step-by-step, and you really will win the race!

▲

Have you ever met a successful person who wasn't restless . . . who was satisfied with where he or she was in life? They want new challenges. They want to get up and go . . . and that's one of the reasons they are successful.

Alex Trebek, TV personality

▼

6. Keep Moving Forward

When I ran in my first marathon, I was afraid that a time would come when I would "hit the wall" and would have to use every bit of strength I had to keep moving. It didn't happen.

But Mount Rainier was a completely different experience. As we made our way up the mountain through a blinding snowstorm, it was all I could do to keep putting one foot in front of the other. I wanted to ask our guides if we could please stop and rest for just a few moments, but they kept pushing us onward and upward. They knew that if we were going to reach our destination we had to keep on moving, no matter how difficult. As a result, I discovered reserves of strength and energy inside of me that I didn't know I had.

When we finally reached Disappointment Cleaver, and I was able to look back and see how far we had come, I was filled with pride because of what I had been able to accomplish. I also realized that it was the journey itself that was important because of what it was showing me about myself. Even if I didn't reach my destination— the summit of Mount Rainier—I was having experiences on that mountain that few others will ever know.

▲

I will take fate by the throat. It shall not overcome me. I shall have the courage of endurance. Where my body fails, my spirit will dominate. My heart will create. I shall speak out of the silence. I shall shout. I shall sing. Man, help yourself, for you are able!

LUDWIG VAN BEETHOVEN

▼

I was discovering the truth of these words from adventurer Harold V. Melchert: "Live your life each day as you would climb a mountain. An occasional glance toward the summit keeps the goal in mind, but many beautiful scenes are to be observed from each new vantage point. Climb slowly, steadily, enjoying each passing moment. The view from the summit will serve as a fitting climax for the journey."

When former Chicago Bears running back Walter Payton died in 1999, the world lost a great athlete and a super human being. One of the reasons for Payton's success on the football field was his philosophy of "having the courage to do things you are not an expert at . . . having the courage to stick with it once you start, and learning from every step you take until your particular goal is reached."

He said, "Even if your goal is never reached, it is a learning process that will enhance your life. Just remember, it is your decision to succeed or fail; no one else's."

One important way you can keep moving forward when you would rather turn back is to keep a positive image of success in your mind. Consultant James Mapes says he learned about the importance of positive thinking while rock climbing on an Outward Bound adventure. Mapes, who doesn't like heights, managed to make his way about three-quarters of the way to the top of a steep cliff, but all of a sudden he couldn't find a fingerhold. He felt desperate, dizzy, and weak. He remembers thinking "I'm going to fall!" He could feel his legs shaking, and thought, "It would be so easy to just let go."

It was at that moment that he recalled something the climbing instructor had said. "See yourself at the top." Summoning all of his inner strength, Mapes formed in his mind a clear, vivid picture of himself standing on top of the cliff looking down. That's when something almost magical happened. Newfound strength and courage flooded into him. In the next instant, he found the fingerhold he needed, and slowly—toe, hand, toe, hand—continued his climb. Soon, he was standing on the cliff, looking down, just as he had pictured in his mind. It was at that time, Mapes said, that he learned about the reserves of courage and ingenuity that become available when we hold a positive image in our minds.

Yes, you can make it to the top! But you've got to keep moving forward to get there!

7. The Only Thing That Can Stop You Is You!

The final thing we need to do, if we want to live large, is to have confidence in our own ability to accomplish and succeed. Most people who never achieve their dreams are not held back by difficult circumstances. They are not thwarted by lack of opportunity or because strong men oppose them. They fail simply because they don't believe they can succeed.

I think there's a bit of Rodney Dangerfield in all of us. He tells of going to his psychiatrist and asking for help in overcoming his inferiority complex. The doctor gave him a quizzical look and then said, "You don't have a complex. You *really are* inferior."

Dangerfield's joke makes us laugh because, deep down inside, most of us are afraid that we really are inferior in some way . . . and that it's only a matter of time before the whole world sees it.

Well, it ain't true! Every human being is made in the image of God, which means that every human being has the ability to accomplish great things! Yes, that means you!

Beethoven was almost completely deaf when he composed many of his best-known works, including his amazing Ninth Symphony. How in the world was he able to do that? Read the quote on page 42 again and you'll see. He was determined that nothing would hold him back, not even his own physical limitations!

Niccolò Paganini, the great violinist, learned about his inner strength in a most unusual way. He was preparing to perform in front of a huge crowd when he suddenly realized that the violin he was holding did not look familiar. Where was the fine craftsmanship? There had been a terrible mix-up and he was stuck with someone else's cheaply made instrument. The concert was going to be a disaster! He was horrified. But the concert had to go on. Paganini began to play.

That evening, he gave the concert of his life. And in his dressing room afterward, he confided to a fellow musician, "Today, I learned the most important lesson of my entire career. Before today, I thought the music was in the violin. Today, I learned that the music is in me."

And the music is in you. And me. God put it there.

Before moving on, I want to share one final story about the importance of embracing failure as a means of learning how to live large.

Dr. Beck Weathers was an accomplished mountain climber. He had already spent ten years scaling many of the world's highest peaks when he decided to make an assault on Everest in 1996. Looking back, he says that he was obsessed with mountain climbing and adds, "I regret the time taken away from my family. . . . There's a large dose of selfishness involved. . . ."

Things changed on May 10. Years before, he had undergone radial keratotomy surgery to correct his nearsightedness. Suddenly, as he neared Everest's summit, the altitude caused the lenses in his eyes to flatten out. He couldn't see! The only thing he could do was stay where he was and wait for help. Surely, when he got back to a lower altitude, his vision would be restored. But suddenly, a blizzard roared in from nowhere. Temperatures dropped to fifty below zero, with winds gusting up to 70 miles an hour. Weathers was trapped, and soon lapsed into a hypothermic coma.

It wasn't until the next day that his fellow climbers found him, covered with ice and barely breathing. There was no way he could survive for more than a few moments longer. They knew that no one has ever come out of a hypothermic coma and lived, so they decided to leave him right where he was. But somehow, Beck Weathers did survive. He revived, got up, and managed to find his way back to camp. When he got there, his face was black beyond recognition from frostbite, and his right arm was frozen in front of him in an eerie salute.

All the experts said that his chances for longtime survival were almost nil, but Weathers continued to surprise everyone. He underwent ten surgeries. The fingers on his left hand were amputated, and so were four fingers from his right hand. Surgeons had to build him a new nose. But despite all of that, Weathers says now that his ordeal on the mountain, as horrible as it was, was the defining experience of his life.

When CBS News asked him if he would like to have his hands back, he said, "Sure. Would I like to have my hands back enough to go back to who I was? No."

He says, "I'm probably a much happier person now, having gone through what I've gone through. I have a different set of priorities. You never know who you are and what you are until you've really been tested. You gain a whole lot more from having failure kicked up from around your ears than success could ever teach you."

He goes on to say, "Even if I knew exactly everything that was going to happen to me on Mount Everest, I would do it again. That day on the mountain I traded my hands for my family and my future. It is a bargain that I readily accept."

In his book *Left for Dead*, subtitled *My Journey Home from Everest*, Weathers writes that on a mountain, "Your body doesn't carry you up there. Your mind does. Your body is exhausted hours before you reach the top; it is only through will and drive that you con-

45

tinue to move. If you lose that focus, your body is a dead, worthless thing beneath you."

He also says, "High-altitude climbers must enjoy putting themselves in situations where they're not sure how they're going to respond. It is one of the most intriguing aspects of this type of climbing. No matter how good you are, you're never sure you can do it. . . . You hope you will be honorable, that you won't fall apart . . . but you don't know until the moment of truth."

"Glass-half-empty people" might say that Dr. Beck Weathers isn't the man he used to be. And he would agree. He knows that it's only now that he's finally learned how to live large!

Are you brave enough to move on up to the next level?

Okay then. Let's go!

T·H·R·E·E

LIFE LESSON NUMBER NINE: LEARN PATIENCE

Perfection is attained by slow degrees. It requires the hand of time.

VOLTAIRE

Lord, please give me patience. And do it quickly.

JUST ABOUT EVERYBODY AT ONE TIME OR ANOTHER

I'M NOT A VERY PATIENT MAN. At least that's my nature. I'm always full of energy. I like to keep moving and I don't like standing still. It bothers me to think of all the time I've wasted waiting in line . . . for the light to change . . . for someone to show up . . . for the basketball season to start . . . for the basketball season to end . . . and on and on. I try to fill up life's little slices of "nothingness" with positive activities. I do push-ups. I write letters. I make phone calls on my cell phone. I take care of paperwork.

If I've got a doctor's appointment, you don't find me thumbing through the three-year-old copy of *National Geographic*. Unless I'm really feeling sick, I'll almost always take a stack of work with me so I can make the most of my time in the waiting room.

To some degree, it was that inner restlessness that drew me to Mount Rainier. I also figured it was that seemingly unlimited supply of energy that would get me to the summit. I'd try to run up the side of the mountain, just the way I had run 26.2 miles in the Boston Marathon.

Wrong!

On a mountainside, in a blizzard, that's a very good way to end up as a frozen grease spot. I found out that it takes patience, patience, and more patience to make it to the top of a mountain. When you find yourself in a situation where the slightest misstep can send you hurtling to your death, you had better spend plenty of time making sure that every step is the right one. That's how it is on a mountain like Rainier. And that's how it is when you're scaling any kind of mountain.

Being decisive is great. Being reckless is an entirely different matter. And if you want to get to the top of the mountain, you had better know the difference!

I'm told that the guides on Africa's Mount Kilimanjaro have a Swahili chant that sets the pace as they move up the mountain: "*Pole, pole!*" It's pronounced po-lay, po-lay, and it means, "Slowly, slowly."

In mountain climbing, and in life in general, there are times when you have to take it slow and exercise caution. Ice is slippery. So is life. That's why it's important to be patient when the situation calls for it. Be aware of the moment. You have to keep listening and looking and sensing your surroundings, because the mountain would just as soon flick you off its back as it would let you succeed in reaching the summit.

One of the best lessons I ever learned about the importance of patience came when I was a twenty-four-year-old hotshot running a minor league baseball team in South Carolina. Less than two years out of college, I had been named general manager of the Spartanburg Phillies, a Class A team. One of the team's owners was a man named R. E. Littlejohn, who had made his fortune in the oil business.

One afternoon, a heavy rain blew into Spartanburg, completely soaking the playing field. The team that was supposed to be in

48

town for a game that evening was three hours away by bus. Naturally, their general manager didn't want to come all the way to town if there wasn't going to be a game. In fact he was looking for a day off and was calling me every half hour or so, pressing me to cancel the game.

It didn't look like we were going to get the game in anyway, so about 2 P.M. I told him just to stay where they were and that I'd cancel the game. Guess what happened almost immediately after I made that decision. That's right. It stopped raining. The sun came out. By game time, the field was completely dry and it was a beautiful evening.

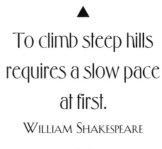

▲

To climb steep hills
requires a slow pace
at first.

WILLIAM SHAKESPEARE

▼

About 6:30 P.M. Mr. Littlejohn showed up with an important businessman from out of town. Only there was no game for them to see. And in addition to the loss of an evening's entertainment was the loss of as many as three thousand paying customers.

Mr. Littlejohn wasn't angry but he was obviously unhappy. "Patience, Pat," he told me. "Go slowly. Don't ever be in a hurry to make a decision about something like this. Haste is only good in catching fleas!"

As usual, Mr. Littlejohn was right.

Anyone who wants to live a successful, satisfying life must learn to practice patience.

That's why the Bible says, "A man's wisdom gives him patience; it is to his glory to overlook an offense." (Prov. 19:11)

The Bible tells us further, in the fifth chapter of Galatians, that patience is one of the "fruit of the Spirit" that grows in those who have truly surrendered their lives to God. And there is no greater example of patience than Jesus Christ, who refused to repay evil

49

with evil, and was always patient, kind, and loving, even to those he knew would eventually turn on him and crucify him. Patience is one of God's attributes, and for me, that alone is reason enough to pursue it.

My friend Jamie Brown once read an article to me that said, "You can make the clock strike before the hour by putting your own hand in it, but it will strike wrong. You can tear the rosebud open before its time, but you will mar its beauty. So we may spoil many a gift of blessing which God is preparing for us by our own eager haste. He is weaving our lives and has a perfect plan for each. Don't pull at the threads!"

In this chapter, I want to tell you how you can climb the mountains in your life by striving to do the following:

1. Walk carefully.
2. Breathe properly.
3. Take as much time as you need to get things right.
4. Pay attention to timing.
5. Take care of yourself.
6. Live in the present.

1. Walk Carefully

As I mentioned earlier, the day before my comrades and I began our assault on Mount Rainier, Heather MacDonald spent several hours with us, teaching us the skills we needed to climb the mountain. She had an awful lot to say about patience, focusing primarily on two important subjects:

▲ How to walk on a mountain
▲ How to breathe on a mountain

Really, these two techniques go together. They involve a mode of travel that will help you get to the top of your mountain without doing unnecessary damage to your body. It all starts with a technique called "rest-stepping."

50

Rest-stepping involves what I call doing a little "jab step." Basically, it is putting one foot in front of you and kicking it into the surface to give yourself solid footing. Then you straighten your rear leg to the point where the bones are in vertical alignment, rest momentarily, and then repeat the process.

Does it sound complicated? It is, at first. You really have to think about what you're doing with every step you take. But if you keep on doing it, it becomes almost second nature. Or at least that's what I thought. More about that in just a moment.

Anyway, rest-stepping helps the climber maintain solid footing on an incline, and it prevents wear and tear on the body by transferring the weight from the muscles to the skeletal structure.

▲

In any contest between patience and power, bet on patience.

W. B. PRESCOTT, PHILOSOPHER

▼

If you've ever seen a *National Geographic* television special on mountain climbing, you've probably wondered why the climbers moved so slowly, almost like zombies in lockstep. Now you know. They were rest-stepping.

Mountaineer Lou Whittaker says, "Climbing Mount Rainier is a lot like climbing stairs. It involves going straight up all the time, as well as switchbacking to the top. In this situation . . . the 'rest-step' becomes vital."

On a mountain like Rainier, one false step can lead to terrible problems. The same is true of life in general. Walk carefully! The Bible admonishes us to "walk circumspectly, not as fools but as wise, redeeming the time" (Eph. 5:15–16 NKJV).

Harriet Rubin, founder of Doubleday Currency, says she has discovered that "you have to go slower to go faster sometimes. I look at competition and I see strength coming out of holding back, not out of going faster."

2. Breathe Properly

The second technique Heather MacDonald taught us was "pressure-breathing." This involves drawing in a short breath through your nose, then blowing it out rapidly through your mouth. If you're doing it right, your cheeks will balloon out as you blow, making you look something like one of the local squirrels with a mouthful of nuts.

Lou Whittaker says, "At really high altitudes, we sometimes take several breaths like this between each step. On Everest, my summit climbers took up to eight pressure breaths between each step as they neared the summit."

He explains, "If you pressure-breathe at sea level, you'll hyperventilate. At high altitude, you can't hyperventilate . . . the atmospheric pressure is too low."

He also says that if you use rest-stepping and pressure-breathing in tandem, "you have a really efficient machine at work. These two techniques have gotten many guides and clients to the summits of mountains all over the world, from Rainier and McKinley to Himalayan beauties such as K2, Kangchenjunga and Mount Everest."

Well, I practiced and practiced these two tried-and-true mountain-climbing techniques until I was sure I had them down pat—no pun intended.

When we started up Mount Rainier the next morning, I was rest-stepping and pressure-breathing with the best of them. Then we made our way around a rock formation that lay in our path. That's when everything changed.

Until we reached those rocks, we had been walking on familiar brown earth and green grass. But ahead of us, everything—and I do mean everything—was dazzling white with snow! It was a whiteout—a condition in which no object casts a shadow, the horizon cannot be seen, and only dark objects are discernible. It looked as if we were going to be walking straight into limbo, and it was frightening!

I knew that we were going to spend that night at a place called Camp Muir, and I figured we'd better get there as soon as possible. My attitude was, *Come on, let's go!* And because I wanted to move fast, I forgot all about rest-stepping and pressure-breathing.

Instead, I headed up the mountain as fast as I could go. But I didn't get very far. After about twenty steps, I was completely fried! I didn't think I could take another step, and I could feel panic raging through me. That's when our guide, George Dunn, caught up with me and pulled me aside. He was polite enough. But he was also very firm.

"Williams," he said, "if you don't do what we told you to do, you've had it." I knew he was telling the truth. I had a vision of myself collapsed in a helpless heap, letting the snow cover me, and I certainly didn't want that to happen!

So we made our way back to the group, and I fell into rhythm with the others—step . . . breathe . . . step . . . breathe . . . step— and so on. As I began to breathe properly, the panic within me started to subside. And the rest-step method of walking carried me slowly but surely through the snow toward my goal.

Don't get me wrong. The next four hours were no picnic! The snow continued to swirl around us the whole time, making it very difficult to see where we were going. And the icy wind seemed to cut right into my bones. But through it all, we kept moving on— step . . . breathe . . . step . . . breathe. And I am convinced that it was only because we were breathing and walking properly that we were able to make it to the safety and relative comfort of Camp Muir.

I discovered that day that there is only one way to climb a mountain, and that is one step at a time, one breath at a time. In other words, slowly!

I also learned another valuable lesson:

Life is not a wind sprint. It is a marathon. There is great truth in the story of the tortoise and the hare. Slow and steady does win the race!

Richard Carlson, author of the best-selling *Don't Sweat the Small Stuff*, has some good advice for those who may be feeling impatient because they want to move faster than circumstances will allow. He writes: "Patience adds a dimension of ease and acceptance to your life. Becoming more patient involves opening your heart to the present moment, even if you don't like it. If you are stuck in a traffic jam, late for an appointment, opening yourself to the moment would mean . . . gently reminding yourself to relax. It might also be a good time to breathe, as well as an opportunity to remind yourself that, in the bigger scheme of things, being late is 'small stuff.'"

If you're moving too fast, you never know what you're missing.

I recently heard about a man named Walter—a minister—who lost his wife, Murtis, to cancer after sixty-four years of marriage. Walter and Murtis had actually known each other for seventy-six years, ever since they met on a playground when they were both ten years old.

Walter had been taken with Murtis from the first moment he saw her and remembers telling one of his friends, "That's the girl I'm going to marry someday." Then, to put into action his plan to win her hand, he wrote her a note that said, "I would like to walk you home after school, but I must clean erasers first. Would you wait for me?"

She responded with a note of her own: "I have to go home, but I'll walk slow."

Obviously, Walter caught up with her.

Seventy-six years later, as Murtis lay in the hospital dying, Walter sat beside her bed, holding her hand. After a particularly long period of silence, she said, "I'm going home now, Walter."

He squeezed her hand. "What do you mean?"

"I'm going home to heaven," she replied, "to be with Jesus. But I'll walk slow."

Once again, I am sure that Walter will catch up with her one day.

▲

Patience is a necessary ingredient of genius.

BENJAMIN DISRAELI

▼

3. Take as Much Time as You Need to Get Things Right

When I first got to Mount Rainier, I was ready to start climbing. I figured that maybe we'd have to spend a couple of hours learning all about our equipment and picking up some mountain-climbing techniques. But then we'd be ready to go. Wouldn't we?

To my great impatience, I discovered that I was wrong. It was going to take more than a couple of hours to get us into proper

54

shape to attack that mountain. The plan was for us to spend an entire day getting ready to make the climb.

I was disappointed by the delay. But looking back on it now, I hate to think about what might have happened to us in that blizzard if we hadn't taken as much time as we needed to make sure we knew how to do things right.

And that's the third thing I learned about patience from Mount Rainier, that it is important to take the time you need to get things right, no matter what anyone else says or thinks.

The great western novelist Louis L'Amour wrote, "The trail is the thing, not the end of the trail. Travel too fast and you miss all you are traveling for."

What would you do if someone called you "a d——d fool"? It would be human nature to think, *I'll show him! Who does he think he is to talk about me that way?* Abraham Lincoln took a vastly different approach, one that saved the lives of thousands of Union soldiers. During the height of the Civil War, Lincoln yielded to tremendous political pressure and signed an order that would have transferred a number of Union regiments from one field of battle to another.

Edwin Stanton, who was Lincoln's secretary of war, refused to carry out the order, stating publicly, "Lincoln is a d——d fool for ever signing that order." Lincoln could have fired Stanton on the spot. Fired him? He probably could have had him shot! Instead, the President said, "If Stanton said I'm a d——d fool, then I must be one. He is nearly always right on military matters. I'll stop over and find out what his reasoning is."

When Lincoln did "stop over," Stanton was able to convince his boss that the order was a terrible one that would result in thousands of additional casualties, so Lincoln rescinded it. Had the President not been a patient man, he would have refused to listen to Stanton and kept the order in force with disastrous results. It might have even turned the tide of the war.

Lincoln knew the importance of taking the time to get things right because he had seen how often forcing an issue brought about an undesirable outcome. He had remarked, "A man watches his pear tree, day after day, impatient for the ripening of the fruit. Let him attempt to force the process, and he may spoil both fruit and tree. But let him patiently wait, and the ripe pear, at length, falls into his lap."

John Ruskin said, "On the whole, it is patience which makes the final difference between those who succeed or fail. . . ."

And John Schiller has said, "Only those who have the patience to do simple things perfectly will acquire the skill to do difficult things easily."

What about you? Will you work on developing the patience you need to "do difficult things easily"?

This is an important part that I wish I could get across to the youth of today. Most of the kids I see are in far too great a hurry to grow up. Do you remember a thing called "adolescence"? It used to be the period of time between childhood and adulthood. It usually started sometime around your twelfth birthday and lasted into the mid- to late-teens.

Not any more.

Now it seems like it lasts for a couple of months at most—if it happens at all. One day, little girls are hosting tea parties for their dolls and teddy bears; the next day they're wearing lipstick and trying to look sexy. Little boys go from innocent, open-faced children to jaded, cynical adults overnight.

It's not supposed to be that way! It takes time to make the successful transition from being a child to being a grown-up. Perhaps that's one reason why there are so many adults in the world today who are acting like children.

I believe that impatience is also affecting the style of play in the National Basketball Association, where too many young players are trying to make the jump straight from high school to the pros. Some players are able to make that transition. Kobe Bryant of the Los Angeles Lakers comes to mind, as does the Minnesota Timberwolves' Kevin Garnett. But these guys are the rare exception to the rule. No matter how good a player may be in high school, he is generally not ready to play professional basketball right away.

He needs to spend some time in college, developing and perfecting his skills first. But too many young guys don't have the patience to do that. They want the big money and the big stardom right now. The end result for some of these young players is that they never develop their full potential—and their professional careers don't last very long.

There are so many ways impatience can hold you back in life. But if you take as much time as you need to make sure you are doing things right, chances are very good that you will go far.

4. Pay Attention to Timing

Did I feel bad that I couldn't make it all the way to the summit of Mount Rainier? Of course, I did. But it would have been foolish for me to say to our guides, "I don't care what the conditions are like. I'm going anyway." Did I say foolish? It would have been suicide! The timing wasn't right and I had to acknowledge that.

Timing is an important ingredient of success. It's one of the reasons why it's necessary to be patient. You're waiting patiently for your opportunity to move. You're like Henry Aaron or Ted Williams, looking for that fastball right down the middle of the plate—for that pitch you can drive over the center field wall!

> ▲
>
> Patience is power. Patience is not an absence of action; rather it is "timing." It waits on the right time to act, for the right principles and in the right way.
>
> BISHOP FULTON J. SHEEN
>
> ▼

I first learned about the importance of waiting for the right timing when I was general manager of the Spartanburg Phillies, working for R. E. Littlejohn, whom I mentioned earlier.

Well, the Phillies had a very good season during that year of 1965, and I just knew some big league team was going to offer me a chance to prove myself at the AA or AAA level. I was more than ready to begin my climb toward the major leagues. But the phone didn't ring.

I can still see the smile on Mr. Littlejohn's face as he put his arm around my shoulder in fatherly fashion. "Patience, Pat. Patience," he said. "You've got to have patience."

He said it so often that I got tired of hearing it. I didn't want to spend another year on the bottom rung of the minor leagues.

"You've got to prove yourself," Littlejohn told me.

"I just did!"

"Well, do it again! And if you have to, do it again after that!"

When I protested, he gave me that same friendly smile. "You know," he said, "anybody can be a one-shot salesman. You've got to go back to the same people year after year, and sell yourself again and again. Sooner or later, the timing will be right and your day will come."

"Pat," he insisted, when he saw the discouraged look on my face, "you can make it all the way to the major leagues from here."

I wasn't sure if he knew what he was talking about. But what choice did I have except to do as he had advised and wait for my day to come? After all, I didn't have any other job offers at the moment.

I stayed at Spartanburg for the 1966 season, and we had another good year. Surely the phone would ring this time.

Wrong again.

But finally, after I had proven myself again and again, the call came. At the "ripe old age" of twenty-eight, I was hired as the business manager of the Philadelphia 76ers. It wasn't baseball, but it was the big leagues, and it was a career move that changed my life.

Somebody says, "Being patient is great, but how do I know when the exact moment has come for me to act?" Only you can answer that question, because every situation is different. But here are three important things to keep in mind:

▲ *No* is a good word. Don't be afraid to use it.
▲ The Boy Scouts are right. It's important to "Be Prepared."
▲ Be willing to take the first pitch.

Here's what I mean.

First, when you're under pressure to make a decision and you're not really sure which way you want to go, say no. Why? Two reasons. Number one, say no because it's easier to change a no to a yes than to do the reverse. In other words, once you've committed yourself to something, you may find it hard—or even impossible—to back out of it without losing face and causing hurt feelings. Number two, say no because if you're not really sure you want to say yes, you probably don't.

Second, be prepared. You never know when the "big moment" is going to come, so be ready for it at all times. As Winston Churchill said, "To every man, there comes that special moment in his lifetime, when he is figuratively tapped on the shoulder and offered the chance to do a very special thing, unique to him and fitted to his talent; what a tragedy if that moment finds him unprepared or unqualified for the work which would be his finest hour."

> ▲
>
> Until you value yourself, you won't value your time. Until you value your time, you will not do anything with it.
>
> M. SCOTT PECK, AUTHOR
>
> ▼

Third, be willing to take the first pitch. In baseball the patient hitters almost always seem to be the better hitters. Some guys can't wait to get up to home plate and start swinging. Such free-swingers tend to strike out more frequently than other more patient batters. They need to learn to lay off the first pitch—to take a little time to size up the pitcher and find out what he's really got. In basketball it's called "taking *your* shot." In other words, make sure you've got a clear shot at the basket from within your range. If not, pass the ball to one of your teammates.

As Barbara Johnson wrote in her book *Where Does a Mother Go to Resign?* "Patience is the ability to idle your motor when you feel like stripping your gears." Wait for the real opportunity, and then hit the ball as hard as you can!

5. Take Care of Yourself

It's a sad story. Tom insisted he wasn't a workaholic. He just wanted to provide for his family—even though he almost never saw them. That's because he was too busy working—twelve to fourteen hours a day, six or seven days a week. He ate on the run. He didn't have time to exercise. He insisted that four or five hours of sleep were enough. He shrugged off the stress and fatigue and said,

"That's the way life is for just about everybody these days." He gave his family all sorts of wonderful things—a beautiful house, a luxury car, a private school for the kids, and lots of money in the bank. Yes, sir, he was doing a great job of taking care of things.

And then he dropped dead of a heart attack at the age of forty-three. You see, Tom was taking care of everything but himself. He was giving his family everything he thought they wanted—but what they really wanted was more of him. And now they had lost him forever.

If you're going to climb the mountains in your life, you simply must take care of yourself. If you do not have sufficient water and food for the climb, and don't take enough time to rest, you'll never make it all the way to the top. So eat right, get plenty of rest, exercise regularly, take time to do some of the things you want to do, and learn to say no to new obligations when you've already got enough on your plate.

It's important to stop every so often and take stock of your life. Prioritize things so you don't devote most of your time and energy to projects you really don't care all that much about. I suggest that you make a list of all the things you're doing that aren't really important to you, or that you really don't want to do, and see if you can figure out how to stop doing them. Then make a second list of all the things that you'd really like to do but aren't doing because you just can't find the time for them.

For example, if you've always wanted to take piano lessons but just don't have the time, look for a way to make time by cutting some other unnecessary and/or unpleasant activity out of your life. Is serving on that committee really so important to you? Do you really need the income from that second job?

It's also important that you take care of your inner self. Pray. Take time to be with God. If you're not involved in a good church, start looking for one right away—a place where you can fellowship with people of faith who can support and encourage you. After all, mountain climbing is a team sport. And so is life.

If you really want to climb a mountain, you have to keep yourself in tip-top shape, physically and spiritually.

I heard a joke about a woman who went for a drive in the country one beautiful Saturday afternoon. She was astonished by the sight of a farmer, holding a goat, and standing on top of a ladder next to an apple tree. When she pulled over to the side of the road for a better look, she could see that the farmer was patiently lifting the goat up so the animal could eat apples from the tree. She got out of the car, walked over to the ladder, and asked the farmer what he was doing.

"Feeding my goat," came the obvious answer.

"But there must be a better way to do it!" she cried. "That seems like an awful waste of time."

"Don't worry about it," the farmer shrugged. "What's time to a goat?"

Well, I never said it was a good joke! Anyway, a lot of people are like that farmer. They spend their time taking care of everyone but themselves. But if you really want to take care of other people, you have to take care of yourself first.

Try to live in accordance with the words of St. Francis de Sales, who said, "Have patience with all things, but chiefly, have patience with yourself. Do not lose courage in considering your own imperfections, but set about remedying them every day; begin the task anew."

Former Giants and Braves manager Clyde King wrote about one of the great lessons he learned through his friendship with Dr. Norman Vincent Peale: "He told me, often, that it was important to be patient with yourself and with others. He said that if I couldn't learn to be patient with myself, I'd never learn to be patient with others. It's been a struggle for me, all my life, to be patient."

I also love these words of wisdom from Victor Hugo: "Have courage for the great sorrows of life and patience for the small ones. When you have laboriously accomplished your daily task, go to sleep in peace. God is awake."

Amen!

6. Live in the Present

What are you going to do today? Whatever your plans may be, let me give you a bit of good advice. Actually, it's not *my* advice. It comes from best-selling author Max Lucado, but I do try to live by it. Lucado writes that every new day is a gift from God to be used wisely and carefully. Because of this we each can join Lucado in making the following assertions each day:

▲ I refuse to be shackled by yesterday's failures.

▲ What I don't know will no longer be an intimidation. It will be an opportunity.

▲ I will not allow people to define my mood, method, image or mission.

▲ I will pursue a mission greater than myself, by making at least one person happy he or she saw me.

▲ I will have no time for self-pity, gossip or negativism . . . from myself or from others.

Wow! Wouldn't it be great if all of us lived that way every single day? Our problems would begin to fade away, and our mountains would be easier to climb because we'd be doing it together, supporting one another every step of the way.

Sadly, it seems to me that many of the people I know are too busy thinking about what happened yesterday or what might happen tomorrow to make the most of the time they have today. The Bible puts it this way: "Do not worry about tomorrow, for tomorrow will worry about itself. Each day has enough trouble of its own" (Matt. 6:34).

▲

Yesterday is dead, tomorrow hasn't arrived yet. I have just one day, today, and I'm going to be happy in it.

GROUCHO MARX

▼

What this means for anyone who's trying to climb a mountain is to keep your mind on what you're doing at this moment. Concentrate on the move you're making right now—on finding the right fingerhold, the exact spot to place your foot. If you're thinking about what you're going to do another 100 yards up the road, you may make a careless move right now, and that can bring disaster.

Again and again as I was climbing up Mount Rainier, I had to remind myself to pay attention to the moment. Yes, I knew the

62

warmth and safety of Camp Muir was waiting for us at the end of our day's climb, but I could not allow myself to daydream about that because a moment of inattention could lead to disaster. Dozens of times during my career in sports, I've seen a good team defeated because they were looking past today's opponent to a game that was coming up next week or next month.

Former Dallas Cowboys' coach Tom Landry had strong feelings about the importance of concentration. He once said: "Concentration is when you're completely unaware of the crowd, the field, the score, other than how it might affect strategy. You're concerned only with your performance, playing well at your position. Golf is an excellent example of concentration. You see a golfer blow a hole, then go bogey on the next two holes. You know his concentration has been broken. When my concentration—as a play-caller, a head coach—isn't broken, I'm never on the defensive. When you start thinking defensively, you think such things as, 'Gee, this field's bad, and we're behind and we're not gonna be in the championship game.' It's difficult to recover then.

"Most people don't realize it, but a great measure of a football player is his ability to concentrate. This is why any team in the NFL can win any game if a superior team isn't concentrating, and this is why Vince Lombardi's teams at Green Bay did so well. Lombardi was a driver who kept his teams concentrating. I've trained myself to concentrate. I blank out everything else. If you do that, you don't show emotion. I trained myself by watching Ben Hogan, who had tremendous concentration. He never let anything break his concentration."

If you want to reach the summit of your mountain, you have to keep your mind on the business at hand right now. A wise scribe named Yelchaninov wrote about the sorrow that comes from failing to live in the present moment: "Our continual mistake is that we do not concentrate upon the present day, the actual hour of our life. We live in the past or in the future. We are continually expecting the coming of some special hour, when our life shall unfold itself in its significance. We do not observe that life is flowing like water through our fingers, sifting like precious grain from a loosely-fastened bag." His words remind me of this passage from the Book of Psalms: "This is the day the LORD has made; let us rejoice and be glad in it" (Ps. 118:24).

Pastor-author Chuck Swindoll reminds us that every day is "a twenty-four hour segment of time never lived before and never to be repeated. You may never live to see another day like this one. You may never be closer to a decision you need to make, a step you need to take, a sin you need to forsake. . . . So—do so today. Before the sun sets and tomorrow's demands eclipse today's desires."

What a difference it would make in most of our lives if we tried to follow that advice! All those mountains that look so impassable to us now would be conquered in no time.

I strive to have the attitude presented in one of my favorite *Dennis the Menace* cartoons. It's bedtime and, as Dennis is being carted off to bed against his will, he asks his mother, "Why is tomorrow always getting here before I'm through with today?" How wonderful it would be to make the most of every moment, instead of "killing time" and looking for diversions to help us pass the hours.

Stanley Marcus, chairman emeritus of Neiman-Marcus department stores, was once asked, "What do the wealthy, powerful, and famous people you know have in common?"

"They all have twenty-four-hour days," he answered. He went on to explain, "The world has expanded in almost all directions, but we still have a twenty-four-hour day. The most successful people and the most unsuccessful people all receive the same ration of hours each day."

One night last year I read this story from the little *Our Daily Bread* devotional: "Do you have a clock or watch available with a secondhand on it? Stop and follow that hand as it ticks away 1 minute. Those seconds, of course, are the way we measure time, and time is the very essence of our lives. By the time you reach the age of 75, the clocks and watches of this world will have ticked away a total of nearly 2.5 billion seconds.

"Bernard Berenson, an internationally famous art critic, had a zest for life. Even when he was in ill health, he cherished every moment. Shortly before he died at age 94, he said to a friend, 'I would willingly stand at street corners, hat in hand, asking passersby to drop their unused minutes into it.' Oh, that we would learn to appreciate the value of time!" (used by permission).

The next day my booklet on leadership arrived from Economics Press and I read these interesting comments on time: "The ticking of the clock is one of the most important things in the world. It marks the passage of time. It reminds us that another second, another hour, another day has gone. And yet, despite this constant reminder, most of us go along using time aimlessly, failing to get out of it either enjoyment of life or the satisfaction of accomplishment.

"We know that the opportunity that today presents will never be repeated; that spring fades into summer, and presently autumn becomes winter, and we wake with a start to realize that another year has passed.

"Still we postpone. 'There is plenty of time,' we tell ourselves. That is the great fallacy."

Wouldn't it be great to live without regrets? To be content in the moment—knowing that you were doing exactly what God had called you to do?

Legend has it that Saint Francis of Assisi was hoeing in his garden one day when a companion asked him, "If you knew that you had only ten more minutes to live, what would you do?"

Saint Francis didn't even have to think about it. "I would keep on hoeing my garden," he said. He was a man who was concentrating completely on the present moment, rather than worrying about what he ought to be doing next, or what had happened yesterday. Perhaps that's one of the reasons why his spirit was so gentle that birds would land on his shoulder, and wild animals such as deer, squirrels, and foxes would gather around him without fear.

By contrast, I'm afraid that most people spend about half of their time lost in the past, indulging in regret and sorrow over what has been lost or mistakes that have been made. The other half they spend in the future, either because they think things will be better when it gets here or because they dread its arrival. Either way, they are missing the present, failing to see that there is really only one moment in which we live, and that moment is now.

You see, the best way to have a great tomorrow is to have great todays!

In one of my favorite movies about baseball, *Field of Dreams*, one of the characters—an elderly doctor named "Moonlight" Graham—is asked what it was like to play one inning as a member of the New York Giants in 1922 and never get a chance to bat.

Dr. Graham's reply: "It was like coming this close to your dreams and then watching them brush past you like a stranger in a crowd. At the time, you don't think much of it. You know, we just don't recognize the most significant moments of our lives while they're happening. Back then, I thought there'll be other days. I didn't realize that that was the only day."

How sad to look back on the biggest moments in your life and realize that you missed them. And sadder still to spend so much time in sorrow over yesterday's lost opportunities that you totally miss out on today.

Shortly after all-time-great college football coach Paul "Bear" Bryant died, his family found a crumpled, yellowed piece of paper in his wallet. From its condition, it appeared that he had carried that piece of paper with him for years and had unfolded and read it many times. It read: "This is the beginning of a new day. God has given me this day to use as I will. I can waste it or use it for good. What I do today is very important because I am exchanging a day of my life for it. When tomorrow comes, this day will be gone forever, leaving something in its place I have traded for it. I want it to be a gain, not a loss—good, not evil, success, not failure, in order that I shall not regret the price I paid for it."

Think you might have some trouble living up to those words? If so, remember that perfect practice makes perfect. Practice just makes permanent. When you fall short, forget about it and make a resolution to try again when the new day dawns. As Ralph Waldo Emerson said: "Finish every day and be done with it. You have done what you could. Some blunders and absurdities no doubt crept in; forget them as fast as you can. Tomorrow is a new day. Begin it well and serenely and with too high a spirit to be cumbered with your old nonsense. This day is all that is good and fair. It is too dear, with hopes and invitations, to waste a moment on the yesterdays."

Before we take our next step up the mountain, I want to give you some words of wisdom from Joe Torre, manager of the 1999

World Champion New York Yankees. Torre, who played eighteen seasons in the National League, writes that he and all-time home run king Henry Aaron were spending some time one day talking about batting slumps, "when he made a comment that's stayed with me ever since. 'Each at-bat is a new day.'"

Torre continues, "No matter what our line of work, we all endure slumps. When we find ourselves in a rut, 'each at-bat is a new day' is a line worth remembering. I'd take it even further: We don't just have the opportunity to start fresh each day. We have the opportunity to start fresh every moment.

"When we take this philosophy to heart, what we're really doing is focusing on the present. We can learn from the past failures and mistakes, but we shouldn't get stuck there. We can keep future goals in mind, but we shouldn't get stuck there either. The only way to reach our potential is to focus on what we must do now . . . at this moment, this day . . . to perform effectively and to win."

Are you ready to move on? The mountain is beckoning!

F·O·U·R

LIFE LESSON NUMBER EIGHT: LEARN TO ADAPT TO CHANGING CONDITIONS

Accept the fact that life is like fording a river; stepping from one slippery stone to another, and you must rejoice every time you don't lose your balance, and learn to laugh at all the times you do.

MERLE SHAIN, AUTHOR

IF YOU DON'T LIKE THE WEATHER on a mountain, just stick around for a few minutes. Chances are, it will change. Sometimes, the changes will come so fast and furiously that you'll be left feeling like you just climbed out of the Teacups at Disney's Magic Kingdom. It's not uncommon for a mountain climber to experience all four seasons in the space of a single afternoon—moving fairly quickly from the blistering heat of summer to the bone-chilling ice and snow of deep winter. I've already mentioned the sudden weather change I encountered on Mount Rainier. Everything was

69

calm and clear one moment, and the next, we were walking into the teeth of a raging blizzard.

And the weather is not the only thing that changes suddenly as you make your way up the face of a mountain. One minute you'll be walking on soft grass; the next you'll be making your way up solid granite. As altitude increases and the air gets "thinner," you're likely to find yourself gasping for breath, when you were doing just fine an hour or so ago.

Anyone who is going to make it to the top of a mountain has to be prepared for changes like these—has to expect them in fact, knowing they will come.

When I first got to Mount Rainier, I figured there really wasn't anything that could stop me from getting to the top of that peak. This climb was merely going to be another accomplishment that I'd add to my growing resume of athletic achievement.

Yeah, right! It's not that I was arrogant. It's just that I didn't know what I was getting myself into!

A few months before heading to Washington State, I had competed in the Boston Marathon. I'd made the final turn down Boylston Street as tears of joy streamed down my cheeks, making my way past thousands of spectators who were cheering me on to the finish line. True, I was hours behind the front-runners. But it still felt to me like I had won a gold medal in the Olympics.

I had come to Mount Rainier with those cheers ringing in my ears, so I was not expecting defeat. But I quickly discovered

▲

Once you begin to think in terms of what should have happened, instead of concentrating upon the situation that confronts you, you're in terrible danger of letting down.

SANDY KOUFAX

▼

70

that there are many differences between running in a 26.2-mile marathon and climbing a 14,000-foot mountain. Here's just one example:

In Boston, two million people lined the streets to watch the race, and the city's residents were wonderful hosts. They shouted out encouragement as we passed by, handed out Gatorade, and manned water stations where thirsty runners (like me) could get the strength they needed to keep on going.

But you know what? Mount Rainier didn't have any of those things. There were no smiling faces urging me on with a friendly, "Way to go! You're doing great!" Nobody was handing out Gatorade or offering a drink of cold water. I could have used all those things!

Even though I was part of a team, it was ultimately up to me to climb the mountain. I had to be willing to push myself to the limits of my endurance, and I had to be ready to adapt to whatever changing conditions the mountain threw at me.

Change comes at all of us from day to day, sometimes at frightening speed.

Those who are ready for change, and can adapt to it, will probably succeed. Those who are unprepared for change or who resist it will most likely fail.

For example, consider the final T in AT&T. As I'm sure you know, it stands for "telegraph," a system that isn't in great demand these days. Imagine what would have happened to this great company if AT&T's board of directors had said, "We don't care about progress. We believe in the telegraph and we're sticking with it—no matter what!"

An attitude like that would have swept AT&T right into the dustbin of history, along with the Acme Buggy Whip Company. But because AT&T's leadership welcomed changing technology, the company remains strong and vital, even in this era of e-mails, the Internet, and satellite communications. The leadership at

71

AT&T understood that change is not an enemy to be fought off but a challenge to be embraced.

Before we go any further, let's take a moment for a quickie quiz:

What do these four men have in common: the apostle Paul, Babe Ruth, Michael Jordan, and Christopher Reeve?

You're right. All of them successfully adapted to major changes in their lives—in some instances, changes that would have destroyed a lesser person.

The apostle Paul is always the first person who comes to my mind when I think about someone who was ready and willing to adapt to change. The first major change in Paul's life occurred on the road to Damascus, where he had a face-to-face encounter with the risen Christ. Suddenly, the man who had devoted his life to hating and persecuting Christians had become a Christian himself!

After that, Paul's life became a real roller-coaster experience. In the eleventh chapter of 2 Corinthians, he put it this way:

> Three times I was beaten with rods, once I was stoned, three times I was shipwrecked, I spent a night and a day in the open sea, I have been constantly on the move. I have been in danger from rivers, in danger from bandits, in danger from my own countrymen, in danger from Gentiles; in danger in the city, in danger in the country, in danger at sea. . . . I have . . . often gone without sleep; I have known hunger and thirst and have often gone without food; I have been cold and naked.
>
> VERSES 25–27

Quite a list, isn't it? And yet in the midst of all this, Paul also wrote: "I have learned the secret of being content in any and every situation, whether well fed or hungry, whether living in plenty or in want" (Phil. 4:12). He knew that changes were bound to come— some good, some bad, and some neither. Whatever came his way, he was ready for it and always made the most of it. In fact, when he wrote those lines about being content, he was in prison. It was from the same dank, dark, dirty prison cell that he reminded Christians: "Rejoice in the Lord always. I will say it again: Rejoice!" (4:4). And: "Finally, brothers, whatever is true, whatever is noble, whatever is right, whatever is pure, whatever is lovely, whatever is admirable—if anything is excellent or praiseworthy—think about such things" (4:8).

Here was a man who didn't let even the most difficult changes stop him from reaching out to change the world for Christ. But what about the three other men I mentioned?

The first, Babe Ruth, started his baseball career as a pitcher, and a very good one. In six seasons with the Boston Red Sox, he won eighty-nine games and pitched twenty-nine consecutive scoreless innings in the World Series. Then he was traded to the New York Yankees, who decided they wanted his bat in the lineup every day and put him in the outfield.

He wasn't comfortable out there at first. He tried hard and developed into an outstanding fielder. He hit 714 home runs in his career, a record that stood until Henry Aaron broke it in 1974. Ruth successfully adapted to change.

And there is Michael Jordan. Did you know that basketball was not Jordan's sport of preference? He loved baseball. But as he kept growing, so did his strike zone. He was an imposing figure at the plate, yes, but he was a frequent strikeout victim.

Reportedly, it was his father who suggested that he try something different—like basketball. That didn't start out so great. Michael was cut from his high school team in his sophomore year, but remembers, "I knew I never wanted to feel that bad again. I never wanted to have that taste in my mouth, that hole in my stomach. So I set a goal of becoming a starter on the varsity." The rest, as they say, is history.

And what about Christopher Reeve? As an actor, he entertained millions of people. He was probably best known for playing the role of Superman in a series of movies. Then a tragic horseback riding accident left him paralyzed. Strapped into his wheelchair, unable to move, he bears little resemblance to Superman.

Yet it's only because of his injury that Christopher Reeve's courage has become known to the world. We have seen his humor in the face of tragedy. He and his wife have given the world a glimpse of what love and devotion between two human beings is really all about. He has become a source of inspiration and encouragement to thousands of people all over the world who share his fate and to millions of others who do not.

Would Christopher Reeve have chosen to spend his days in a wheelchair, unable to move his arms and legs? Of course not. But for whatever reason, that is what happened, and he is making the most of it.

But how can you come to the point where you are not caught off guard and swept off your mountain when conditions change dramatically? Three ways:

1. Sharpen your focus.
2. Pay attention to the little things.
3. Work hard.

1. Sharpen Your Focus

We were above the 10,000-foot level on Mount Rainier—slugging our way through knee-deep snowdrifts somewhere between Camp Muir and the summit.

Suddenly, our guide, George Dunn, hollered, "Crevasse!"

What was that? I wondered. I didn't see anything. What on earth was he talking about?

▲

The first requisite for success is the ability to apply your physical and mental energies to one problem, incessantly, without growing weary.

THOMAS EDISON

▼

Then I saw it. Saw it? I almost stepped in it, and it would have swallowed me up. I had never seen a crevasse before, and my first encounter with one left me shaking in my crampons. It was a huge hole that seemed to go down forever—like the "bottomless pit" the Bible talks about in the Book of Revelation.

And that was how I learned about the importance of focusing on the task at hand—no matter what that task may be.

Have you heard the story about the dumb . . . er, brunette who stood for hours staring at a carton of orange juice in her neighborhood grocery store? When someone finally approached her and asked what she was doing, she pointed at a word written on the back of the carton: CONCENTRATE.

Well, maybe the woman in that joke isn't as dumb as she sounds, because absolute concentration and focus is a key to success in life. Here are five specific ways you can strive to sharpen your focus and thus propel yourself toward the summit of your mountain:

▲ Focus on the next step.
▲ Focus on what you want to do—not on what you don't want to do (in other words, stay positive).
▲ Keep your eye on the ball (avoid distractions).
▲ Concentrate on one thing at a time.
▲ Use performance cues.

First, *focus on the next step.*

As we saw in the last chapter, it's very easy to fix your attention on the future or the past. When you do that, you are not able to make the most of the present moment. When you are not focusing on what you are doing right now, the unexpected can catch you completely off guard.

Naturalist John Burroughs said, "The lesson which life repeats and constantly enforces is, 'look under your foot.' You are always nearer the divine and the true source of your power than you think. The lure of the distant and the difficult is deceptive. The great opportunity is where you are. Do not despise your own place and hour. Every place is under the stars; every place is the center of the world."

Because I was not concentrating on my next step, I was very nearly swallowed up by a crevasse. However, after that, I could have begun looking out for crevasses to the point where I neglected to see other dangers (or opportunities) in my path. Don't worry about what happened two steps back. Don't spend your time worrying about what might be waiting for you fifty steps up the road. Instead, concentrate on the step you are taking right now! As Thomas Carlyle said, "Our grand business is not to see what lies dimly, in the distance, but to do what lies clearly at hand."

The legendary Ben Hogan, considered by many to be the greatest golfer of all time (before Tiger Woods arrived on the scene, that is), attributed his success to his ability to focus completely on every

75

swing. Said Hogan, "To me, concentration is the business side of golf. Swinging the golf club is incidental."

Or as motivational speaker Art Turock put it, "Focused action beats brilliance any day."

Second, *focus on what you want to do instead of what you don't want to do*. In other words, keep your attention riveted on the steps you need to take to reach your goal. Don't focus on the mistakes you might make that could keep you from reaching that goal.

Well into his seventies, Karl Wallenda was still thrilling audiences with his death-defying feats on the high-wire. Even a family tragedy, in which two were killed and several were seriously injured, could not coax him into retirement. He announced to the world that he was going to walk on a wire stretched between two ten-story buildings in downtown San Juan, Puerto Rico. Unfortunately, Wallenda's focus had changed. His wife said later that the family tragedy had caused his goals to shift. She said that as he prepared for the event in San Juan, "All Karl thought about, for months, was not falling."

As writer J. Allan Peterson wrote, "Unwittingly, he had broken the cardinal rule of goal-setting, by focusing on what he didn't want to happen rather than what he did." Thus, as thousands watched, Karl Wallenda plunged to his death. Peterson goes on to say, "All our goals must be directed toward the positive, the productive, the excellent, the godly." Otherwise, there will be no way to stand strong when the winds of change are blowing.

Third, *avoid distractions*.

A reporter once asked Babe Ruth this question: "How is it that you can come up to bat in the bottom of the ninth, in a key game, with the score tied, with thousands of fans screaming in the stadium, with millions listening on the radio, the entire game on the line, and deliver the game-winning hit?"

Ruth's answer, "I don't know. I just keep my eye on the ball."

An understatement? Perhaps. But then again, perhaps not.

Pitcher Robin Roberts, who won 286 games during 19 major league seasons from 1948 to 1966, said, "I think much of the reason nerves never bothered me when I pitched was that I was able to concentrate so well on the mound. I just stood out there, in total isolation, focused on throwing the ball as well as I could. Nothing bothered me and I was oblivious to even the batter. When I was throwing well, I would only see the bat when he swung, my concentration was so centered on the catcher. As far as I was concerned, the ball was going to the catcher, not the batter."

How do you develop that kind of concentration? It takes time, effort, and plenty of practiced self-discipline.

Jerry Potter, writing in *USA Today*, tells of the time Phil Mickelson shot a practice round of golf with Arnold Palmer: "When they reached the 18th tee, Mickelson noticed Palmer was angry. 'I thought I had done something wrong,' Mickelson said. 'Then he walked over to the side of the tee and said: "Right there! That's where it happened."'" Palmer went on to explain that, in 1961, a fan had congratulated him on winning the Masters. He shook the man's hand; then made double bogey on the 18th hole to lose to Gary Player, by a stroke.

"For Mickelson, it was a lesson in staying focused. For Palmer, it's a painful reminder of costly mistakes."

Potter quotes Palmer as saying, "I knew it was the wrong thing to do. . . . I lost my concentration."

Palmer's contemporary, Jack Nicklaus, said that he became a champion by learning how "to immerse myself in a cocoon of concentration." Fellow golfer Ken Venturi said of Nicklaus, "You can go up to him at the first tee and say, 'Jack, your house is burning down,' and he'll say, 'I'll take care of it when I get in.' I don't think Jack Nicklaus has ever been distracted."

One word of caution, though. It is possible to overdo it with the concentration. I found this out when my daughter Caroline and I were jogging through our Orlando neighborhood. Out of the corner of my eye, I saw a woman on a bicycle but I was too focused on running to even notice who she was. A short time later, our paths crossed again, and this time I was shocked when she stopped her bike and started yelling about how rude I was.

I stopped running and looked up into the angry face of one of our neighbors. "You are so rude!" she shouted. "You don't even have enough manners to say hello!" She said a lot more too while I stuttered and stammered and tried to explain that when I'm running, I'm so focused on what I'm doing that I don't notice anything else. Finally, my offended neighbor accepted my apology, and

I went on my way, realizing that there are times when it's okay to be distracted.

Fourth, *concentrate on one thing at a time*.

A couple of summers ago, we remodeled our house. If you've ever done anything like that, you know what an ordeal it is—a summer full of noise, dust, and clutter, and an unsettled, uncomfortable feeling that would never really let you relax.

The last part of the job was converting one large room into three bedrooms and a bath. The entire job was accomplished by one man—a wiry, little guy named Alan—in the remarkably short time of six days. You should have seen Alan go! He practically ran through his days, and when I asked him why he worked alone, he replied that other people would just slow him down.

When the job was finished, I asked him to tell me his philosophy: "I stay focused on one job until it's finished," he said. "I work as fast as I can and as well as I can. I don't want to float around from one job to another. You can't work efficiently that way."

Thomas Edison was once asked what he considered to be the first requisite for success. His answer: "The ability to apply your physical and mental energies to one problem incessantly." When pressed to explain his answer, the great inventor said, "You do something all day long, don't you? If you get up at seven and go to bed at eleven, you have put in sixteen good hours—and it is certain, with most men, that they have been doing something all the time. The only trouble is that they do it about a great many things, and I do it about one. If they applied it in one direction, they would succeed."

The fifth aspect of focusing that will help you climb your mountain is the use of *performance cues*.

Performance cues are simple, short, positive reminders about the goals you are striving to accomplish. Motivational coach Shane Murphy has had much success teaching Olympic athletes how to use performance cues to increase their concentration. For a skier a performance cue might be doing something as simple as reminding herself to keep her hands forward. For a tennis player it might be a self-reminder to keep his arms extended.

Murphy says that effective performance cues should be decided on well in advance of pressure times, broken down into short actions that will help you focus, and rehearsed often.

Performance cues are very helpful to me in my career as a public speaker. Every time I speak to a new group of people, I realize that it may be my one chance to get my message across to them, and I want to make a lasting, positive impression. To help ensure that this happens, my performance cues include keeping my level of enthusiasm high, doing stretching exercises for my shoulders and neck, and ensuring that my shirt and pants are clean and pressed. I also make sure that I'm properly hydrated and that I've had a throat lozenge. Last, but certainly not least, I check my teeth to make sure there's no spinach stuck between them. Otherwise, my audience might remember me for the wrong reason!

▲

Don't be afraid to give your best to what seemingly are small jobs. Every time you conquer one it makes you that much stronger. If you do the little jobs well, the big ones tend to take care of themselves.

DALE CARNEGIE

▼

2. Pay Attention to the Little Things

The second thing you must do to withstand the sudden changes that occur on the mountain is to take care of the little things.

That means making sure you get plenty of rest, stay hydrated, and eat twelve small meals a day to keep your energy level high. It means making sure your equipment is in good shape so it can withstand adverse conditions. It means making sure you have everything you need to cope with whatever conditions may arise on the mountain. But it also means that you are not carrying extra equipment that will weigh you down unnecessarily.

Failure to pay attention to the little things can cost you dearly if you're trying to get to the top of a mountain—or do anything else in life. Former NFL quarterback Phil Simms says, "When you get tired of doing the little things, it will show up on the field. . . . Players lose interest before they lose talent. They've had enough. They're tired of grinding it out every day. They're tired of the little things."

You have to take care of the little things if you want to stay in tip-top physical shape—or spiritual shape. Jesus said that paying attention to the little, seemingly insignificant matters leads to spiritual growth and maturity. He said, "You have been faithful in a few things; I will put you in charge of many things" (Matt. 25:23).

Does it seem like I'm overstating my case? Syndicated columnist Sydney J. Harris used some baseball statistics to point out just how important those "little things" can be. "Consider two major league baseball players. One hits .275 for the season. The other hits .300. The one who hits .300 may easily have a contract awarding him twice as much as the one hitting .275; yet, the difference between the two, over the season, is only one extra hit in forty times at bat."

Paul S. Goldner, in his book *Red Hot Cold Call Selling*, recalls a year in the 1960s when golfer Jack Nicklaus won $400,000 on the PGA tour—a tremendous amount of money for that era. During the same year, a golfer by the name of Bob Charles won around $40,000—only a tenth of what Nicklaus had picked up. Does that mean Nicklaus was ten times the golfer Charles was?

Hardly. Goldner writes, "It might surprise you to learn that the difference in their respective per round stroke average was less than half a stroke. Imagine that! The difference between the greatest golfer of all time and a very good golfer was less than half a stroke per round."

Basketball legend Kareem Abdul-Jabbar is another person who became a winner by paying attention to the small details. He said, "I try to do the right things at the right time. They may be just little things, but they usually make the difference between winning and losing." He led the Los Angeles Lakers to three NBA championships.

The old song says, "Little things mean a lot." Here's some evidence that it's true:

▲ In 1645 one vote gave Oliver Cromwell control of England.
▲ In 1649 one vote sent Charles I of England to the executioner.
▲ In 1776 one vote saw to it that English was declared the official language of the United States. Had that vote gone the other way, we would all be speaking German!

▲ In 1845 one vote gave statehood to Texas.

▲ In 1868 President Andrew Johnson was spared from impeachment by one vote.

▲ In 1876 one vote changed the government of France from a monarchy to a democracy.

And there's more:

▲ In 1876 one vote gave Rutherford B. Hayes the presidency of the United States.

▲ In 1933 one vote gave Adolf Hitler the leadership of the Nazi Party in Germany.

▲ In 1960 one vote change in each precinct in Illinois would have given the presidency to Richard Nixon.

Baseball great Ted Williams, my boyhood idol, once complained that he had received a defective box of bats. He said they didn't feel right—the handles were faulty—and he sent them back to the manufacturer. The company did some tests and discovered that Williams was right. The new bats were off by five one-thousandths of an inch.

I was present at the Ted Williams Museum when he accepted the donation of a bat that he had reportedly used in 1941, when he became the last major league baseball player to hit over .400 in a season. Williams took the bat in his hands, closed his eyes, and started squeezing the handle.

Then he nodded his head, "Yeah, this is one of my bats. In 1940 and '41 I cut a groove in the handle of my bats to rest my right index finger. I can still feel the groove. It's one of my bats all right."

Wow! Talk about paying attention to the little things.

Now, some people have accused me of making too big a deal of taking care of life's small details. They say I'm striving for perfection, and perfection is impossible. Well, if even 99.9 percent of perfection were good enough, here's what would happen:

▲ 2 million documents would be lost by the Internal Revenue Service this year.

81

▲ 22,000 checks would be deducted from the wrong bank accounts within the next 60 minutes.

▲ 12 babies would be given to the wrong parents every day.

▲ More than 1,300 telephone calls would be misdirected every minute.

▲ More than 100,000 income tax returns would be processed incorrectly every year.

▲ More than 800,000 credit cards would have erroneous information on their magnetic strips.

▲ Some 200,000 wrong drug prescriptions would be written in the next year.

▲ More than 100 incorrect medical procedures would be performed within the next 24 hours.

▲ And 315 entries in *Webster's New International Dictionary* of the English language would be misspelled.

When Lou Holtz was football coach at Notre Dame, he said, "If two seminars were held at the same time, one conducted by a successful team and one by a losing team, the similarities between the two would be amazing." He went on to say that both of the teams would approach the game the same way. They would probably spend about the same amount of time on the practice field.

"The main difference would be attention to detail. In the successful organization, no detail is too small to receive attention. No job is minor, and everyone takes great pride in realizing they are important and their responsibilities are critical to the unit's success."

I love this story about Michelangelo: A friend who was visiting the great artist asked to see how his latest sculpture was coming along. What he saw surprised him. "I can't see that you have made any progress since the last time I was here," he said.

Michelangelo vehemently disagreed. "I have made much progress," he said. "Look carefully, and you will see that I have softened the lines here." He went on to explain that he had retouched this part, reworked that part, and so on.

The visitor was bewildered. "That may be," he said. "But those are all trifles."

Michelangelo smiled patiently. "But trifles make perfection," he said. "And perfection is no trifle."

As John Chancellor, former anchor for NBC News, said, "Genius lies in the details."

Even though it goes against current thinking, I like this sign I saw in front of a radio station in Jacksonville, Florida: "Pay attention to details. Sweat the small stuff."

There are so many wonderful stories about the importance of paying attention to small details, but I'll content myself with two more. The first has to do with the great scientist George Washington Carver, who invented an amazing array of useful products from plants like peanuts and sweet potatoes.

Carver loved to tell how he came to unlock so many wonderful mysteries from such a simple plant. He said, "When I was young, I said to God, 'God, tell me the mystery of the universe'; but God answered, 'That knowledge is reserved for Me alone.' So I said, 'Then, God, tell me the mystery of the peanut'; and God said, 'George, that's more nearly your size,' and He told me." We never know what amazing discoveries are within our grasp, if only we will learn to look for them.

The second story comes from Bill Walton, television basketball analyst, who played college ball for the legendary John Wooden at UCLA. Walton remembers the first time he and a group of other freshman recruits met with Coach Wooden. They were nearly breathless with anticipation as they waited for the words of wisdom that were sure to drop from the great coach's lips.

Walton and the others were astounded when Coach Wooden held up a pair of athletic socks. "Gentlemen," he said, "I'm going to show you how we wear our shoes and socks." Was Coach Wooden teasing them? No. He was perfectly serious. He went on to explain that he wanted the socks to be smoothed out just so, in order to prevent blisters from forming. He wanted the laces on the shoes to be tied just right. He wanted every small detail to be taken care of so there would be no distractions on the court in the middle of a game.

Did it work? It must have. After all, Coach Wooden's Bruins won a record ten NCAA championships, including seven in a row from 1967 to 1973. He holds the longest winning streak in NCAA

83

history at eighty-eight games in a row. During those years, players came and players went, but the Bruins kept on winning despite all those lineup changes. New defenses were designed, old offenses were discarded, and still, the Bruins kept on winning. It really is true. If you take care of the small details, you'll be able to withstand the forces of change that come against you.

3. Work Hard

Even though I did not make it all the way to the summit of Mount Rainier, I have to tell you, that mountain beat me up five times worse than the Boston Marathon did. When you're on a mountain, you have no choice but to work as hard as you possibly can. If you want to make it all the way to the top, you've got to work hard. If you want to get back to the safety of your base camp, you've got to work hard. The only alternative is to just give up, lie there, and let the snow cover you up—which it will.

▲

If people knew how hard I worked to get my mastery, it wouldn't seem so wonderful after all.

MICHELANGELO

▼

St. Augustine said that people ought to pray as if everything depended on God, but work as if everything depended on them. I like that. I think it strikes just the right balance. If I expect God to give me the desires of my heart, then I had better be working hard to meet him halfway there. I won't, of course. God always does the vast majority of the work, but he expects me to do what I can.

A few months back, my wife, Ruth, and I were visiting son Bobby in Statesboro, Georgia, and we decided to go for an early-morning jog. We were running through a quiet residential neighborhood when Ruth suddenly exclaimed, "Look at that street sign."

I looked where she was pointing and discovered that our jog had carried us to the corner of "North Easy Street." What do you know—there really is an Easy Street. But only in Statesboro, Georgia. The rest of us are going to have to work hard to reach our dreams!

During my years in the National Basketball Association, I've often been surprised to see the work ethic exhibited by players who have already taken their place among the best in the league. These guys had it made. Surely, they didn't need to work so hard anymore. But they did it anyway.

I remember Larry Bird saying after a grueling season that he was going to take a couple of weeks off and then get back to work in an effort to improve his game—which was already far beyond outstanding. He said, "I'll come back next year and have four or five new moves, and they won't be able to stop me." That was in a year the Los Angeles Lakers had defeated the Boston Celtics for the NBA championship, and Bird said, "Watching the Lakers celebrate in our building was horrible. I've been working all year to get that memory out of my mind."

When Bird's seven-year-old son Connor said to him, "Dad, you're famous, or something crazy like that," Larry said, "No, we're normal people who work hard to make a living." Said *Chicago Tribune* writer Sam Smith: "They can put that on Larry Bird's plaque in the Hall of Fame."

Coach Hubie Brown often talks about the work ethic demonstrated by Kareem Abdul-Jabbar. In 1972 Brown was hired as an assistant coach by the Milwaukee Bucks. He was so excited that he wanted to be the first person to arrive at the gym, so he reported to work four hours early. To his surprise, Jabbar was already out there on the court, practicing his sky hook.

Brown was amazed that a man who had been selected as the league's most valuable player two years in a row, and who had led the league in scoring both times, should be working so hard to get better. But that's exactly what he was doing.

And there's a footnote to Brown's story: "Before the other players arrived, Abdul-Jabbar left the court. He didn't want them to know he practiced three hours before the scheduled team practice, because it implied that they should have done the same. He did it all season."

Paderewski, the renowned pianist, said, "If I don't practice for a day, I notice it. If I miss two days, my critics notice it. If I miss three days, the world will know it."

Michael Jordan said, "I never believed all the press clippings and I never found comfort in the spotlight. I don't know how you can, and not lose your work ethic. I listened. I was aware of my success, but I never stopped trying to get better."

Disney CEO Michael Eisner said, "I've learned that it's never the first effort, or the second, or even the third that results in excellence."

There are four things you should know about hard work and how it will help you withstand the winds of change. Hard work:

▲ Beats talent almost every time
▲ Almost always leads to success
▲ Helps eliminate regrets
▲ Increases the likelihood of personal satisfaction and happiness

Now let's look at these principles one at a time, starting with the fact that *hard work beats talent almost every time*.

According to the *Los Angeles Times*, a five-year study of 120 of America's top artists, athletes, and scholars turned up the fact that these people were successful, not because of their great talent, but because they had drive and determination.

Researcher Benjamin Bloom of the University of Chicago said, "We expected to find tales of great natural gifts. We didn't find that at all. Their mothers often said it was their other child who had the greater gift." The *Times* goes on to say, "The researchers heard accounts of extraordinary drive and dedication through which, for example, a child would practice the piano several hours, daily, for seventeen years, to attain his goal of becoming a concert pianist."

▲

If life seems like it's all uphill . . . you must be reaching your peak.

TOM WILSON, CARTOONIST

▼

James E. Byrnes, who served as secretary of state under Harry Truman, felt that the difference between "average" people and "great" people could be summed up in three words: "And then some." He said, "The top people did what was expected of them, and then some. They were considerate and

86

thoughtful of others, and then some. They met their obligations and responsibilities fairly and squarely, and then some. They were good friends to their friends, and then some. They could be counted on in an emergency, and then some."

Byrnes felt that the people who stand out in any field of endeavor are the ones who meet their obligations, and then some. They may not have more talent than their colleagues, but they were willing to work harder in order to achieve their goals.

Superstar singer Celine Dion comes from a large family. One of her brothers recently said that Celine was not the most gifted in her family. She was, however, the one who was willing to work the hardest to achieve her dream of stardom. Hard work paid off for Celine Dion, and it will pay off for you too.

Another important aspect of hard work is that *it almost always leads to success.*

Writing in the *New York Opera Newsletter*, Nancy Stokes Milnes, wife of renowned baritone Sherrill Milnes, tells about a time when she and her husband were having dinner with a well-known voice coach. She wrote, "We played a recording of Sherrill when he was in college and asked that coach, 'What do you think about this voice?' He said, 'Oh, there's not a chance. Don't encourage this person. Tell him to get a day job.'" When they revealed that the voice on the tape was Sherrill's, the coach said, "I'll never discourage another singer."

Mrs. Milnes went on, "The most gifted person can walk into your studio and achieve little. Someone whose talent seems just okay can work and work, until he or she can make it. You can't tell people what their dreams are, or what the limits of their dreams should be. It's up to them to tell you."

Does hard work guarantee success? No, it doesn't, not in mountain climbing or any other endeavor. But as Gerald R. Ford said, "The harder you work, the luckier you will get. Never be satisfied with less than your very best effort. If you strive for the top and miss, you'll still beat the pack."

Nancy Hogshead, the great Olympic swimmer of the 1980s who is now an attorney in Jacksonville, Florida, recently told me that she regularly swam 12 miles a day in preparation for the Olympics. She knew there was no shortcut to success. The only way she could

87

get to the top of her sport was to work, work, and work some more. Was it worth it? Certainly, she said. Why? "Because the rewards of reaching for excellence truly are profound. I'm not talking about a pay raise, a plaque, or even a gold medal. It's living into a purpose or a calling that enlivens even the most mundane tasks. It's a deep pride in the life we are living."

I like what advice columnist Ann Landers said: "Opportunities are usually disguised as hard work, so most people don't recognize them." And as baseball's Maury Wills said, "Luck" is "opportunity meeting preparation."

The third thing hard work does is *eliminate regrets*.

Nancy Hogshead also told me that when she was a girl, her parents "knew nothing about swimming, but they knew a lot about not quitting and hard work. They told me that any activity is fun at the beginning and the finish, but it's the long middle section that's hard. They instructed me that what you start, you finish, because you are either going to face the pain of discipline or the pain of regret. There are lots of reasons to quit anything, but hard work isn't one of them."

It's hard work climbing a mountain. Especially when an icy wind begins to blow, or a wet, cold snow begins to fall. But you've got to keep on moving, pushing ahead toward your goal. If you don't, you will regret it for the rest of your life.

Listen to what John Havlicek told the Indiana University basketball team prior to their national championship game in 1976: "I've never heard of anyone being accused of over-hustling. After this game is over, you don't ever want to have to look back on any situation and tell yourself it might have been different if only you had tried a little harder. In the course of your lifetime, you might live seventy years. These are just two hours out of those seventy years, but they're two hours you'll never get back again. So reach down deep inside and make them two of your very best hours.

"I'm not guaranteeing anything . . . because things don't always work out the way we think they're supposed to. But you'll have a much better chance of success with this approach. Don't ever look back and think: 'I might have had that rebound, if I'd just tried harder.' Don't walk off that court tonight with the feeling you could have given more. Give it all you've got."

88

Wow! Great advice for mountain climbers and other folks who are trying to withstand life's storms. No wonder Indiana won the game.

The fourth thing you need to remember about hard work is that it *increases the likelihood of personal satisfaction and happiness*.

Bart Starr, who had such a great career with the Green Bay Packers playing under legendary Coach Vince Lombardi, remembers that Lombardi demanded "that every player on his team be committed to excellence . . . use his God-given talents to the fullest. . . ." Starr says this was a philosophy Lombardi taught his players to apply, not just on the football field, but in life. "He told us: 'The quality of any man's life is in direct proportion to his commitment to excellence,'" Starr says, adding that he will always remember those words, which go hand-in-hand with these from author-philosopher Ayn Rand: "A man of limited ability who rises by his own purposeful effort, from unskilled laborer to shop foreman, is a career man in the proper, ethical meaning of the word . . . while an intelligent man who stagnates in the role of a company president, using one-tenth of his potential ability, is a mere job holder."

Before we move on, I have two final thoughts about hard work.

First, consider the swallows. Did you know that every March hundreds of these little birds fly 6,000 miles over the ocean, from Argentina all the way back to San Juan Capistrano, California? They can't swim. And they can't fly 6,000 miles without stopping.

How do they do it? Each swallow carries a large twig in its mouth. When the birds get tired, they drop their twigs into the water, land on them, and rest until they are ready to resume their flight. Those little birds have worked awfully hard, yes. But they've also planned ahead. And without that, all of their work would go for nothing.

The final thought comes from Ross Perot: "Most people give up just when they're about to achieve success. They quit on the one-yard line. They give up at the last minute of the game, one foot from a winning touchdown."

Don't you be guilty of that. Don't give up now! The summit is in sight!

F·I·V·E

Life Lesson Number Seven: Control What You Can Control and Forget the Rest

Ain't no sense in worrying about things you got control over, 'cause if you got control over 'em, ain't no sense worrying. And there ain't no sense worrying about things you got no control over, 'cause if you ain't got no control over them, ain't no sense in worrying about them.

Mickey Rivers, former Major League baseball player

THERE ARE MANY THINGS on a mountain that no human being can control. That's a lesson I learned very quickly on Mount Rainier. You can't control the weather. You have to take it as it comes—blistering heat or freezing cold. You can't control the terrain. It may be slushy mud that swallows you up to your ankles or

91

a sea of tiny volcanic cinders that withstand your every attempt to find traction.

You can't control the atmosphere. The higher you go, the thinner that atmosphere is going to be, and the more difficult it will be to catch your breath. You can't control the difficulty of the climb. All the wishing in the world won't produce a set of stairs leading up to the summit or transform a 30-degree angle into level ground.

But even though all of these things are beyond your control, you can adapt to them. You can make sure you have the training and the equipment you need to make it all the way to the summit. You can do your best to ensure that you're in good shape physically—that you have the stamina and the strength for the climb. You can stop for rest whenever possible and you can take along enough food and water for the duration of your journey.

Even though you can't control the weather, you can control what effect it has on you—at least to some degree—by dressing appropriately. You can be prepared for the terrain by wearing the proper shoes and having the equipment you'll need. You can be prepared for the angle of the slope and the thinning atmosphere by practicing pressure-breathing and rest-stepping. Or, in extreme conditions, you can carry oxygen with you.

As I was pushing through the snow, heading toward the 10,000-foot level on Mount Rainier, I had plenty of time to think. The first thing I thought was, "What in the world am I doing out here on this mountain?" After that, my thoughts turned to my mentor and old friend R. E. Littlejohn. I often think of him because he taught me so much when I was a young man working for the Spartanburg, South Carolina, Phillies.

> ▲
>
> If you can't change your fate, change *your attitude.*
>
> AMY TAN, AUTHOR
>
> ▼

When I first went to Spartanburg, I worried about a lot of things that were far beyond my control, like the weather. Time after time, we would plan a big promotion for our ball club on a certain day, only to see the day under a threat of rain. Mr. Littlejohn would tell me, "Pat, you can't do anything about the weather, so don't worry about it!" And he was right, even though I had a very hard time taking his advice.

I also worried about the quality of the team we put on the field, even though our roster was completely out of my hands. We were a Philadelphia Phillies minor league team, so it was the people in Philadelphia who made those decisions, not me.

Mr. Littlejohn would say to me, "Pat, you're wasting your energy when you worry about things like that. Instead, you ought to be focusing on the things you can control. You can make sure that our ballpark is clean and comfortable—an enjoyable place for people to come for an evening. You can make sure that our staff is friendly and courteous. And you can do your best to see to it that we serve the very best hotdogs in all of South Carolina."

No wonder, as I trudged through the snow, with icicles beginning to form on my eyebrows, that I thought of my old mentor and his admonition:

Don't worry needlessly about things you can't control or change.

And then I thought about how much of everyday life is beyond our control—just like my situation in the middle of that blizzard. In order to reach the top of your mountain, I believe there are several important things you'll need to understand regarding what you can and can't control in life. They are:

1. You can't control everything that happens to you but you can control your attitude.
2. That out-of-control feeling is nothing new in this world of ours.
3. In today's world change is coming faster than ever before, so be prepared.
4. Setting goals can keep you headed in the right direction.
5. When all else fails, be flexible.
6. When you can't change anything else, sometimes you just have to change yourself.
7. Yes—God is still in control of the universe!

93

1. Control Your Attitude

Up on Mount Rainier, I couldn't do anything about the ice and snow. Nor could I do anything about the pace at which our guides were taking us through that ice and snow. Cursing and grumbling wouldn't have done me one bit of good. All I could do was summon up my inner strength and try to remember what Heather MacDonald and George Dunn had taught me about mountain climbing.

I also took comfort from the fact that what I was going through at the time—no matter how unpleasant—was actually good for me because it was making me stronger. That's the sort of attitude you have to have to get to the top of any mountain—an attitude that is willing to learn from disappointments, setbacks, and failures as they happen, and then turn them into strength and wisdom for the future.

Not too long ago I had the privilege of visiting with an elderly gentleman who has lived in the Orlando area for more than eighty years.

"Eighty years!" I said, "Imagine that. I'll bet you've seen some amazing changes during that time."

"Yes, I have!" he agreed. "And I've been opposed to every dadblasted one of 'em!"

Well, you know, that's just how some people react whenever anything "different" or "unexpected" comes along. That's why Woodrow Wilson said, "If you want to make enemies, try to change something."

I've also heard about the prayer offered up by the minister when his congregation was making an important policy decision. "Lord," he prayed, "please help us to be right about this. Because if we're wrong, we'll probably keep doing it the wrong way for the next hundred years." He knew how resistant to change people can be. Once a policy was instituted, it wasn't likely to change, no matter what.

It's sad that so many people react to change, or any momentary setback, with a negative, whining attitude. Again, such an attitude will not—cannot—do you any good. Instead, the proper attitude is to ask yourself questions like, What can I learn from this that will help me next time? How can I turn this situation to my advantage? How do I need to adjust my thinking or my actions in light of these changing circumstances? Rather than focusing on temporary setbacks, it is vital to try to see the big picture, to keep a long-range perspective.

I believe it would be impossible for me to overstate the importance of maintaining a positive attitude.

A positive attitude involves being willing to cooperate with others. It involves cheerfulness. It involves being courteous. It involves entering every situation with a desire to build up instead of tear down. For me, it involves this prayer: "Lord, help me to be constructive in everything I do."

Unfortunately, a positive attitude can be rather hard to come by these days. I got a taste of that when I was stuck in a horrendous traffic jam in a tunnel. It was miserable in that tunnel to begin with. For one thing, it was the middle of summer, and it was stifling in there. For another, the tunnel was full of gas fumes.

And then attitude came into play. People started leaning out their windows, shaking their fists and shouting threats to other motorists. They began leaning on their horns, as if that would magically make the situation better. Instead, negative attitude was doing what it almost always does—taking a bad situation and making it worse.

Charles Kettering was not the first to observe, "The men whom I have seen succeed best in life have always been cheerful and hopeful men, who went about their business with a smile on their faces, and took the changes and the chances of this mortal life like men, facing rough and smooth alike as it came."

If you have a negative attitude when you're trying to climb a mountain, you'll be fortunate if you make it more than a couple hundred yards beyond base camp. So do yourself a favor. Control your attitude. Keep it positive.

2. That Out-of-Control Feeling Is Nothing New

If you're one of those people who long for the good old days, when life was simpler and people felt more in control, I want to let you in on a little secret. Those days never existed.

I hope it's a comfort to you to know that life today isn't much different than it's always been when it comes to the average person feeling out of control. Certainly the pace of change has accelerated, as we'll see in just a moment. But for humankind, life has always been a constant battle for control, and it always will be. There have always been mountains to climb.

Did you know that Socrates once complained that sports were being ruined because athletes were becoming professionals? He also had harsh words about the younger generation of his day, fearing that they were becoming disrespectful to their elders and lacked moral guidance.

Think things are more difficult in today's world? Archaeologists got a surprise when they translated an Egyptian hieroglyphic dating from the time of Christ. Why? Because the author was complaining about his salary! He said it left him in trouble in the summer and the winter. Sound familiar?

▲

The art of life lies in a constant readjustment to our surroundings.

OKAKURA KAKUZO, BUSINESSMAN

▼

I'm sure you've heard of the Pony Express, that legendary group of cowboys who carried the United States mail across the Western frontier. Do you know how long the Pony Express was in business? Slightly over a year and a half. That's when it was put out of business by the invention of the telegraph!

How many Western movies have you seen with stagecoaches in them? Well, did you know that the stagecoach was used as a means of transportation for only about a decade—from 1858 to 1869—before being replaced by the transcontinental railroad?

96

Rapid change, it seems, is nothing new. Neither is resistance to that change.

In 1829 Martin Van Buren, who was then governor of New York, sent this appeal for help to President Andrew Jackson: "The canal system of this country is being threatened by the spread of a new form of transportation, known as 'railroads.' As you may well know, railroad carriages are pulled at the enormous speed of 15 miles an hour by engines, which, in addition to endangering life and limb of passengers, roar and snort their way through the countryside. The Almighty never intended that people should travel at such breakneck speed."

The automobile met with even more vehement opposition. The folks who manufactured buggies and buggy-connected merchandise worked feverishly to drive the fledgling car makers out of business. They persuaded clergymen to preach sermons against "automobilitis," a "disease," which they said was destructive to religion and personal morals. The Tennessee state legislature even passed a law that anyone who intended to drive an automobile had to put an advertisement in the newspaper to warn pedestrians at least a week in advance.

When the horseless carriage continued to grow in popularity despite all their efforts against it, the "buggy people" convinced several prominent brain surgeons that riding in cars would drive people insane. Doctor Winslow Forbes wrote: "When these racing motor cars reach 30 miles per hour, they must drive themselves, for no human brain is capable of dealing with all the emergencies that may arise should that rate be maintained for any period worth thinking of. The human animal is simply not destined to travel 30 miles an hour; neither the human brain nor the human eye can keep pace with it."

When Robert Fulton first unveiled his new invention, the steamboat, the world was skeptical. According to reports of the day, the crowd that gathered on the shore to watch Fulton's maiden voyage chanted together, "It will never start! It will never start!" But when it did start, churning through the water at an amazing rate of speed, the chanting quickly changed to, "It will never stop! It will never stop!"

The railroad, the automobile, and the steamboat—all three brought tremendous progress to our world. Yet all three produced public fear and ridicule. People couldn't accept them because they were too different, too frightening. People were fearful because life was moving at such a rapid pace. It seemed out of control.

Then, as now, people who resisted these changes were left behind. The carriage manufacturers went out of business. So did companies that made buggy whips and other peripheral items. But those who accepted and adapted found that their lives did not get worse but better.

Can you imagine what our life would be like today if Henry Ford had said, "What's wrong with the horse and buggy?" Or what if Thomas Edison had said, "Candles are just fine"? Thank goodness for those who are willing to step out of their comfort zone and let life get a little wild and wacky sometimes. I like what Anne Morrow Lindbergh said: "Only in growth, reform and change, paradoxically enough, is true security to be found."

It may surprise you to know that, of the one hundred largest companies in the United States at the start of the twentieth century, only sixteen were still around at the beginning of the twenty-first. What happened to the eighty-four companies that are no longer with us? Most likely, they became stagnant, more interested in safety and security—in other words, in feeling "in control"—than in being on the cutting edge of innovation and change. But you don't have to go back to 1900 to see what happens when companies do not change with the times. Of the five hundred companies listed in the Fortune 500 index for 1970, one-third of them were gone by 1985. These were companies that failed to understand, as Gail Sheehy said, "Changes are not only possible and predictable, but to deny them is to be an accomplice to one's own unnecessary vegetation."

Here are some "famous last words" from people who failed to grasp the changes that were headed their way:

> This telephone has too many shortcomings to be seriously considered as a means of communication. The device is of no value to us.
>
> WESTERN UNION INTERNAL MEMO, 1876

98

I think there may be a world market for maybe five computers.

THOMAS WATSON, CHAIRMAN OF IBM, 1943

I have traveled the length and breadth of this country, and talked with the best people, and I can assure you that data processing is a fad that won't last out the year.

EDITOR IN CHARGE OF BUSINESS BOOKS FOR PRENTICE HALL, 1957

But what is it good for?

IBM ENGINEER, COMMENTING ON THE MICROCHIP, 1968

There is no reason anyone would want a computer in their home.

KEN OLSON,
FOUNDER OF DIGITAL EQUIPMENT CORPORATION, 1977

The concept is interesting and well-formed, but in order to earn better than a "C," it must be feasible.

YALE UNIVERSITY MANAGEMENT PROFESSOR, RESPONDING TO
FRED SMITH'S PAPER PROPOSING OVERNIGHT PACKAGE DELIVERY—
SMITH WENT ON TO FOUND FEDERAL EXPRESS

One more: In 1972 Gary Boone, then a young engineer working for Texas Instruments, came up with the idea of a full computer on a single chip, something that would later be developed as the microprocessor. Although Boone was able to get a patent for his invention, he couldn't get his colleagues at Texas Instruments to take him seriously.

Finally, through much persistence, he was able to get a meeting with one of his company's officers. The executive listened politely while Boone shared his idea. Then, with a condescending smile on his face, he asked, "Young man, don't you realize that computers are getting bigger, not smaller?"

3. Change Is Coming Faster Than Ever Before

Walk into any Hallmark store and you can buy a greeting card that plays a tune when you open it. Cute, right? But hardly earthshaking. Well, did you know that single birthday card contains almost as much computing power as ENIAC, the first programmable computer ever built? And ENIAC was 10 feet tall, 80 feet across, and weighed 30 tons! Now, take another look at that card that plays "Jingle Bells" or "Happy Birthday," and see if you don't find it worthy of just a little bit more respect!

We are living in a world full of technical marvels, and the rate of change is increasing on a daily—and sometimes hourly—basis! Consider the car you drive. According to Dean Eastman, director of Argonne National Laboratory, your automobile probably has greater computational ability than the Apollo 11 spacecraft, which took Neal Armstrong and Buzz Aldrin to the moon in 1969!

▲

Today, changes come fast . . . and we must adjust our mental habits so that we can accept, comfortably, the idea of stopping one thing and beginning another, overnight.

DONALD M. NELSON,
BUSINESS EXECUTIVE

▼

And there's more: Three years ago the Internet had 100,000 sites. Today it has nearly 4 million. Last year, while the United States Postal Service was delivering 100 billion pieces of mail—and that's an awful lot of mail—the Internet delivered 4 trillion e-mail messages! Within the next half hour alone, 154 million e-mail messages will be sent!

You say, "Well, Pat, that's pretty amazing all right, but what does it have to do with me?" Simply that it is important for you—and me—to understand that we live in a world of constant change and flux. There is nothing we can do to alter that, no matter how uncomfortable we may be, or how much we may feel nostalgic for the halcyon days when things were simpler.

The truth is you cannot climb a mountain if you are afraid to leave the security of a safe shelter. As Robert J. Kriegel and Louis Patler write in their book *If It Ain't Broke—Break It,* "Things will never get back to 'normal' because unpredictability and change are normal. There is no going back. Get used to it. Change will be followed by more change. . . . The waves in the ocean won't flatten out; they're only going to get bigger and come at us faster."

Jeremy Rifkin points out in his book *Time Wars* that even today's "labor-saving devices" are causing us to work harder. People take their cell phones with them to restaurants, stores, and the theater, so they won't miss an important call. Some people carry portable fax machines with them everywhere they go—even to the mountains or the beach. Most of us are doing all we can to squeeze every drop of productivity out of every hour—all of this in an effort to stay on top of things and maintain control. Robert Staub says, "The pace is accelerating and the race does, indeed, seem to be going to the swift."

Sometimes—especially when I pick up my morning newspaper and read about all the horrible things people are doing to other people in these opening days of the twenty-first century—I begin to wonder why God didn't create us in such a way that we had no choice but to obey him. He could have made it so we are always nice, polite, obedient creatures.

But then I realize there would be no freedom in that kind of universe. And so God put us into this world with its constant change and unpredictability, and it is as we grapple with the change and unpredictability that we grow and are changed for the better.

Anatole France said, "All changes, even the most longed for, have their melancholy; for what we leave behind us is a part of ourselves. We must die to one life before we can enter into another." John F. Kennedy said, "Change is the law of life, and those who look only to the past or the present are sure to miss the future."

What does it take to cope in a world where changes seem to be coming at us faster and faster every day, where things seem to be increasingly beyond our ability to control them? Three things:

▲ First, *the ability to cast off old ways of thinking.* As Donald Nelson says, ". . . we must assume that there is probably a better way to do almost everything. We must stop assuming that a thing which has never been done before cannot be done at all."

▲ Second, *an acceptance of change.* Dr. Martin Groder says, "Embracing change is healthy." He adds that it is important to view change as a normal course of events, "not as an emotional sneak attack."

101

▲ Third, *the ability to be as comfortable as possible in a world where many things are plainly beyond our control.* Helen Peters, of the Hagberg Consulting Group, writes, "Those who can tolerate ambiguity and make decisions in the face of uncertainty will rise to the top."

If your life seems out of control, if changes are happening too fast for you, here are some things you need to keep in mind.

▲ Change happens, so expect it.
▲ People who refuse to change will stagnate.
▲ The quicker you let go of the "old way" of doing things, the sooner you can move on.
▲ Open your arms to change, but don't let go of your values.
▲ Every change causes temporary discomfort, even if the change is something you've always wanted.
▲ Don't expect one or two changes to bring you to your ultimate goal. Every change that you make is simply another step toward that goal. (Remember, success in life is not a destination, but a journey.)
▲ Get ready for the next change. It's coming!

▲

A climbing technique: planning ahead, so that you can anticipate the difficulties and work out the best way of solving them.

ALAN BLACKSHAW, EDUCATOR

4. Setting Goals Can Keep You Headed in the Right Direction

When you're climbing a mountain, your primary goal—obviously—is to get to the top. If you're climbing a small hill and a couple hundred yards will get you to the top, that one goal may be enough. But if your destination is the summit of a mountain like Rainier, you've got to break down that ultimate goal into a series of lesser goals. Think of goals as being like signposts along the way. As I mentioned earlier, it's important to control the things you can and then refuse to worry about the rest. Setting goals is an important means of helping you maintain control of what you can and should control.

When I set out to climb Mount Rainier, my goals might have looked something like this:

▲ Get myself into the best possible shape for the climb.
▲ Make arrangements for the trip to Washington State.
▲ Be certain that I have the training and equipment I need to climb the mountain.
▲ Manage to make it safely to Camp Muir.
▲ Go on the rest of the way to the summit.
▲ Get back down the mountain safely.

If I had been trying to climb Everest, there would have been many more goals involved, most of them having to do with getting from one camp to another, each camp being at a higher elevation than the last. You can't climb Everest in a day or two, so you have to have a series of smaller goals to let you know how you're progressing on your journey.

Jim Collins, rock climber, researcher, and writer, suggests these goal-setting strategies for all varieties of mountain climbers.

▲ First, *make sure your goals are consistent with your values*. No matter how rapidly the world changes, some things must remain the same: honesty, compassion for others, faith. These three qualities have always been important and always will be.
▲ Second, *set goals that are consistent with your abilities*. Collins says, "Unsuccessful mountain climbers—and regular folks who fail to reach unrealistic goals—often fall into the trap of setting goals based on bravado rather than on self-knowledge." He adds, "Good goals are set with self-understanding; bad ones are set with bravado."
▲ Third, *set long-term goals too*. Don't confine yourself to short-term thinking. Collins advocates going as far as setting goals

regarding where you want to be thirty years from now and then breaking them down into five-year increments. And, of course, those five-year goals could be broken down further into one-year goals, and so on.

Collins says the reason some people never get to where they want to be in life is that "they only have base camps (small goals) and never identify the mountain they're headed for."

▲ Fourth, *expect to stumble or fall, but get back up when you do.* In mountain climbing, as in every other endeavor, the only people who don't stumble from time to time are those who aren't trying very hard. As I found out when I was with the Spartanburg Phillies, you can't always tell who the best infielders are by looking at their fielding averages. Sometimes it's the players who take more chances, and who are able to cover more ground, who make the most errors. But they're also the players who make things happen, the kind of guys you want on your team.

To Jim Collins's list of goal-setting strategies, I would add these:

▲ *Make sure your goals are clear and specific.* If your goals are nebulous, the results are likely to be nebulous too. And it probably means you haven't put enough time into thinking about what you really hope to accomplish and how you want to go about accomplishing it. My own personal feeling is that if you can't state your goal in one clear, understandable sentence, then you need to take another stab at it.

▲ *Write down your goals.* There's something about writing things down that makes them more "real." Writing them down also forces you to follow the "clear and specific" rule we've just discussed. Furthermore, if your goals are written down, you can pull them out from time to time and check your progress toward accomplishing them.

▲ *Your goals should have a specific deadline attached to them.* Almost as important as what you're going to do is when you will do it. For example, I have a friend who starts every year by writing down what he hopes to accomplish during that year. He confessed to me recently that he's been writing down some of the same goals every year since 1993. He feels good when he writes them down, and he really does mean to accomplish them, but it never happens. No matter how grand your personal goals may be, if you don't have a realistic timetable attached to them, you may find that you never achieve them at all!

▲

Change is inevitable.

Growth is optional.

JOHN MAXWELL, AUTHOR

▼

▲ *And finally, include God in your goal setting.* What do I mean by this? Two things. (1) Spend time in prayer, seeking to ensure that the goals you've set for yourself are consistent with God's will for your life. (2) Make sure your goals include service to God and his kingdom.

5. When All Else Fails, Be Flexible

Ask any pastor what statement he fears most, and he'll probably answer, "That's the way we've always done it." That rallying cry of the inflexible has stood in the way of progress for hundreds, if not thousands, of years.

I recently read about a congregation that had to hire a new minister when their long-time pastor retired. It didn't take the members of that church long to become annoyed with the new guy, because he started making changes in the order of worship and how church affairs were handled. The critics came out in full force when he hired a man to take care of the extensive church grounds.

The budget committee decided to hold a special meeting to discuss the matter.

"We see that you have hired a gardener," the chairman said.

"That's right," replied the minister, "and he does a wonderful job."

"Perhaps you were unaware that our previous pastor took care of the grounds himself."

"Oh, yes, I knew that," the minister smiled.

"And?" came the challenge.

"And I called him," the young pastor said. "But he doesn't want to do it anymore."

You can bet that with a pastor like that, the congregation had to learn to be flexible in their thinking.

I also had to be flexible in *my* thinking when George Dunn told me there was no way I was going to make it to the top of Mount Rainier. Certainly I was disappointed. I had come 3,000 miles to climb that mountain, and now I was being asked to turn around and go home without attaining my goal. But I knew that conditions were treacherous, and I would have been risking my life if I had insisted on pushing on up the mountain anyway. When you're trying to climb a mountain, you've got to stay loose, roll with the punches, be flexible.

▲

Some of your hurts

you have cured,

And the sharpest you

still have survived,

But what torments

of grief you endured

From evils which

never arrived!

RALPH WALDO EMERSON

▼

In her book *If Life Is a Game, These Are the Rules*, Chérie Carter-Scott says, "Flexibility allows you to be ready for whatever curve lies ahead in life instead of getting blindsided by it."

She goes on to tell what happened in 1967, after Swiss scientists patented the digital technology for making watches. Most Swiss watchmakers rejected the new technology in favor of the gears, ball bearings, and mainsprings they had always used. After all, they reasoned, Switzerland had been noted as the world's leading manufacturer of watches and clocks for more than one hundred years, so why change? Unfortunately for thousands of Swiss watchmakers, a Japanese company called Seiko picked up the digital patent and ran with it. Almost overnight, Japan became the world's leading watch manufacturer.

Over the next few years fifty thousand Swiss watchmakers were forced out of business by the digital technology. It took several years for the Swiss to regain their position in the marketplace, with the advent of the Swatch watch. This story shows clearly why

"We've always done it this way" doesn't work, and why flexibility is so important.

There are a number of ways to get to the top of almost any mountain. Experienced climbers will tell you that one way is usually better than the others, but not always. It depends on changing conditions. Perhaps there is heavy snow in one area and not in another. Landslides might make one path inaccessible.

I'm sure you've heard it said that if you keep on doing things the same old way, you're going to get the same old results.

If you want a new and better result to an old problem, you'd better try a new approach to solving it.

Sometimes changing conditions will require a change in your approach, even though your current approach has been wildly successful. Consider IBM. In the decade between 1980 and 1990, IBM had an average annual profit of over eight billion dollars. In 1990 the company made nearly eleven billion dollars. No other business had ever been so successful. IBM was on an incredible upward spiral that seemed likely to go on forever.

And then everything changed. The era of the mainframe came to an end and the era of the personal computer began. PCs were being purchased almost as fast as they could be manufactured. Over the next four years, as IBM was struggling—eventually, successfully—to reinvent itself, the company lost twenty-three billion dollars! More flexibility sooner and IBM might have been spared that horrendous financial loss. Less flexibility in the face of a changing market and IBM might have gone out of business.

Maintaining a flexible attitude is liberating because it frees you from the constraints of the past. It also frees you from unnecessary worry. On February 20, 1962, John Glenn became the first United States astronaut to orbit the earth when Friendship 7 was launched from Cape Canaveral. But ten times prior to that historic morning, the launch had been scheduled and then postponed due to poor weather conditions or other problems. I don't know about you, but if I had been in Glenn's place, I would have been almost crazy with anticipation. But he remained cool, calm, and flexible.

"I learned, very early in the flight-test business," he said, "that you have to control your emotions . . . you can't let things throw you or affect your ability to perform the mission."

Glenn obviously knew something that I have since discovered: At least 90 percent of the time, the things I worry about never happen. And even if they do happen, the worry has almost always done more damage to me than the thing itself. Flexibility allows you to put worry where it belongs—out of your life—because you know that if one path is closed to you, you can find another one to get you to wherever it is you want to go.

6. Sometimes You Just Have to Change Yourself

Someday I hope to make my way back to Mount Rainier for a second attempt on the summit. I don't expect it to be any easier then. It certainly won't be a shorter trip from the base to the summit. The climb won't be any less strenuous. The weather may not cooperate. Who knows? It may be snowing again.

▲

> Everyone thinks of changing the world, but no one thinks of changing himself.
>
> LEO TOLSTOY

▼

But next time I'll have a better idea of what to expect. I'll know what it takes to get all the way to the summit. I'll be better prepared. I will have grown in my understanding of how to climb a mountain. I'll be a wiser and more confident mountain climber. I will have changed.

If you can't change the mountain, or the conditions on the mountain, you've got to change yourself in order to reach the summit. As Mahatma Gandhi said, "Let us become the change we seek in the world."

And consultant James Mapes advises, "Learn to change your perspective and creativity explodes."

Most human beings are creatures of habit, whether or not they realize it. Even those who pride themselves on their spontaneity probably do most of what they do the same old way, time after time after time. It's not easy to change.

Paul Friedman, editor of the *Pryor Report*, uses three ten-second exercises to demonstrate the powerful pull of habits. I urge you to try them yourself and see if you are typically resistant to change. First, he asks his "guinea pigs" to interlace their fingers. Then, he asks them to notice which thumb is on top. Now, he tells them to interlace their fingers again, but this time with the other thumb coming out on top. Most people have to think carefully about what they're doing, and it just doesn't feel right.

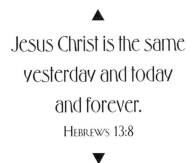

Jesus Christ is the same yesterday and today and forever.

HEBREWS 13:8

Next, he asks everyone to cross their arms across their chest. Again, one arm goes naturally on top. Have you tried it? Now, reverse the order. Was it hard? How long do you think it would take you to get to the point where the second position came naturally?

Finally, Friedman asks everyone to clap hands, paying attention to which hand is "the clapper," and which receives the clap. Then, he says, "continue clapping, but reverse the role each hand plays." If you tried this, you probably discovered that it feels and sounds different.

As you can see, even the simplest changes do not come easily. Personal change comes only with the greatest of effort, but it is almost always worth the effort. Writer Maya Angelou says she will never forget some words of wisdom given by her grandmother: "Sister, there are people who went to sleep last night, poor and rich, white and black, but they will never wake again. Those dead folks would give anything at all for just five minutes of this weather or ten minutes of plowing. So you watch yourself about complaining. What you're supposed to do, when you don't like a thing, is to change it. If you can't change it, change the way you think about it."

7. God Is Still in Control of the Universe!

It's important to remember that even though the mountains change, the One who made them will remain the same forever.

In the midst of a world that seems to be changing with every tick of the clock, God is the same as he was thousands of years ago. He'll be the same thousands of years from now!

And even though he doesn't change, he's not caught off guard by any of the changes you and I may be going through. He is still very much in control of his universe and ready to respond in love whenever we call on him.

I remember an old *Peanuts* cartoon where Snoopy is looking up at the stars and taking great comfort in the fact that they will always be there. Suddenly a falling star appears! Snoopy retreats to his doghouse, completely demoralized.

The stars won't last forever. Mount Rainier won't last forever. This earth won't last forever. But God's love and faithfulness will endure forever!

David Fisher, chapel leader for the Toronto Blue Jays, says that in this world, "Everything seems to be in a state of change. In this flurry of change, we look for stability, reliability, trustworthiness and constancy. A faithful, changeless God is the only One who provides this."

And baseball executive Frank Wren says: "God gives the abilities to make decisions, but I can worry only about what I can control. As long as I realize that it's all in the Lord's control, I don't let the little things bother me."

The very best way to cope in a world that sometimes seems to be out of control is to know the One who holds everything—including you and me—in his hands!

Now, let's move on to Life Lesson Number Six. It's time to join the team!

Life Lesson Number Six:
Be a Winner and
Join the Team

No man is an island, entire of itself. Every man is a piece of the continent; a part of the main.

JOHN DONNE

A MIDDLE-AGED BUSINESSMAN from Ohio, a slightly younger man from Michigan, a husband-wife team from Wisconsin, and me— a guy from Florida, where the existence of mountains is just a rumor—this was our team.

We didn't have much in common. Most of us didn't know very much at all about mountain climbing. We had never met until the day before we began our assault on Mount Rainier. But on that mountain, the five of us strapped ourselves together on one rope. And, under the tutelage of Heather MacDonald, we became a unit. Heather taught us to work together as if our lives depended on it— because they did. For example, we learned how important it was to communicate with each other by means of a simple tug on the rope, hand signals, or facial expressions.

As long as we worked together, Heather told us, we would be fine no matter what the mountain might throw at us. If one of us stumbled or fell or ran into some other type of difficulty, the others would be right there to pick him or her up—as long as we were working together as a team. As the Bible puts it, "Two are better than one, because they have a good return for their work: If one falls down, his friend can help him up. . . . A cord of three strands is not quickly broken" (Eccles. 4:9, 12).

Whenever I talk about teamwork, someone is sure to ask me, "Pat, does everybody have to have a team?"

"Absolutely."

Why? Because it's almost impossible to make it in this world without a team, that's why. We all need people to support us, work beside us, stand with us when times are tough, and share the happiness when we achieve our goals. Former Major League pitcher Goose Gossage once said, "You can't believe what you can accomplish if you pull together as a team."

I think of an acquaintance of mine, a well-meaning pastor of a large church, who seems very likely to run himself into an early grave. He has a number of assistants and associates but he seems unable to delegate. Someone must have told him a long time ago, "If you want to get something done right, you have to do it yourself." That's exactly what he's trying to do—everything, by himself. He doesn't understand how desperately he needs the support of his team.

Someone else says, "But I'm a stay-at-home mom. Surely I don't need a team."

Sure you do! Your team should consist of other moms who have children the same age, so you can share experiences and thus build your mothering skills. Your team includes your children's teachers, doctors, dentists, babysitters—all the people you can count on at a moment's notice.

Everybody needs a team!

In mountain climbing, as in life, the drive for personal glory must be set aside for the sake of group accomplishment. There is tremendous power in teamwork. As someone has said, "The power of the waterfall is nothing but a lot of drips working together."

At the 1914 World's Fair in St. Louis, a man was selling ice cream as fast as he could dip it up—until he ran out of bowls. In a booth next to him a man was unsuccessfully selling a flat confectionery wafer. Noticing the ice cream man's dilemma, the confectioner quickly reshaped this product into a funnel that would hold ice cream, and *through teamwork,* the first ice cream cones were sold!

As I travel across the country giving motivational talks, I've discovered that corporate America wants to know how to build a successful team. It doesn't matter if my audience is made up of executives from Pepsi-Cola, thousands of employees from General Motors, or a small group of folks from a Mom-and-Pop Widget Factory, "team-building" is the number one topic of interest.

A few years ago, I started some serious research on the subject of teamwork as I prepared to write a book, *The Magic of Teamwork.* I contacted dozens of people from all over the country who had demonstrated that they knew how to build effective teams. I asked them to share their strategies with me and I saw quickly that most of them listed eight important characteristics of outstanding teams.

Here, then, are eight things that every team-builder should strive to do to build a winning unit:

1. Look for talented individuals to be on your team.
2. Be a great leader for your team.
3. Make a total commitment to your team.
4. Be passionate about the goals of your team.
5. Think "we" instead of "I."
6. Empower the individual members of your team.
7. Build trust and respect.
8. Build and model character.

Now let's take a closer look at how you should apply these eight principles to the building of your team.

1. Look for Talented Individuals to Be on Your Team

Whenever legendary college basketball coach John Wooden was asked what he looked for when recruiting players for his teams at

UCLA, he had a three-word answer: "Talent, talent, talent." No wonder Coach Wooden's teams won ten NCAA championships!

Still, I think Coach Wooden would have to admit that his tongue-in-cheek answer—as good and as clever as it may have been—was just a wee bit lacking. Suppose Coach Wooden had gone out and recruited five extraordinary ball-handlers, none of whom could shoot a lick. They could dribble that ball for all it was worth and throw accurate behind-the-back passes anytime they wanted to. But when it came to taking the ball to the hole—uh-uh. Just couldn't do it. Or what if he had gone out and recruited the five best centers in the country? No point guards, no shooting guards, no power forwards—just centers. It wouldn't matter how talented those guys were, they'd never win because they didn't have the right mix of talent.

You see, everyone on your team will not have the same responsibility or the same function. That's why the first thing to do is assess your needs. Decide whom you need on your team, and then look for talented people to fill those roles.

How do you judge talent? There's no surefire answer to this one. Consider Mike Piazza. He's almost certainly going to wind up his baseball career as the greatest-hitting catcher of all time. He seems a cinch for the Hall of Fame. And yet, when he made himself available for baseball's amateur draft, nobody seemed to want him. Hundreds of other players were chosen before the Dodgers got around to drafting Piazza—and when they did, it was primarily because he was manager Tommy Lasorda's godson! If judging talent were an easy thing to do, Piazza probably would have been the first player selected—and every singer signed by a major record label would have a number one hit. It just doesn't work that way.

> ▲
>
> What coach, with any instinct or passion for winning, would field an Olympic swimming team or gymnastic team or a Super Bowl team that wasn't made up of the absolute best available talent?
>
> JACK WELCH,
> GENERAL ELECTRIC CEO
>
> ▼

114

There are some things you can do to assess the ability of the people you're considering for spots on your team. You look at a person's experience, examine his or her record, listen to what others say about the person, talk to the person yourself, and then make your decision carefully—very, very carefully.

After all, a wrong decision can be costly. It's estimated that hiring the wrong team member in a corporate environment can result in a loss of up to fifty thousand dollars. So even though there is no surefire way to judge talent, it's important to be as thorough as you can possibly be.

It's also important to look for people who are as coachable as they are talented. What does it mean to be coachable? I'll explain by telling you about a conversation I had with my son Bobby after one of his baseball games at Rollins College. He asked me if I had heard any news about one of his old teammates from high school—a young man with incredible talent who seemed destined for a long and productive professional career.

My son was surprised when I told him that I had, indeed, talked to some major league scouts about his old friend, and they had said they weren't sure if any big league teams would take a chance on him.

Bobby was incredulous. The kid was loaded with talent. Yes, the scouts agreed with that but they saw an attitude that led them to believe he might not be willing to listen and learn. He seemed to think he knew it all already. In other words, he was perceived as not being coachable. And there's no room on any team for someone who is not coachable.

Former NBA coach Chuck Daly had this type of individual in mind when he cautioned, "Teams win championships, not individuals. The players must have ability, but it's essential that they perform as a team."

To be successful, you must have a good mix of people who are willing to do whatever it takes to win, and who don't mind seeing other people get the glory every once in awhile. As English classical scholar Benjamin Jowett said, "The way to get things done is not to mind who gets the credit for doing them."

After Hideo Nomo threw a no-hitter for the Los Angeles Dodgers in 1996, then-Dodgers General Manager Fred Claire said

115

▲

A leader is one who knows the way, goes the way, and shows the way.

JOHN MAXWELL, AUTHOR

▼

that his star pitcher "never talks about individual accomplishments. He always says he wants to be part of a winning team. He means it."

In Japan, where Nomo was a superstar before coming to the United States, players talk about "wa," which means a willingness to set aside personal feelings and goals for the good of the team. This world of ours could use a lot more "wa."

Look for the most talented people you can find for your team, yes. But do your best to make sure that every individual chosen is someone who understands the concept of teamwork, who is willing to learn, and who isn't out for his or her own individual glory.

2. Be a Great Leader for Your Team

I'm not going to take much time right now to talk about leadership—not because it isn't important, but because it's so important I'm going to spend all of chapter 7 talking about it.

During my years in professional sports, I've come to see that the best leaders are those who inspire confidence in their teams.

- ▲ They are trustworthy.
- ▲ They care about the people on their teams.
- ▲ They're exhorters.
- ▲ They are cheerleaders.
- ▲ They're not afraid to see other people get the credit.

They are good leaders because people want to follow them, not because someone else has handed them the authority!

Good leaders show that they have confidence in their people.

116

Sometimes, leaders will even have to take risks to demonstrate their confidence in their people. Jurgen Schrempp, former CEO of Daimler Benz, which is now a part of Chrysler, is a good example of this. Several years ago, Schrempp was climbing in the Italian Alps with noted mountaineer Reinhold Messner. As they were descending a steep cliff, Schrempp was unable to find a good handhold and soon found himself clinging with his fingers to the wall. He was connected by a rope to Messner, who was on solid ground above him. So he shouted out and asked his companion what would happen if he simply leapt away from the mountain into thin air. Messner answered that he would catch Schrempp with the rope and lower him to safety.

Keep in mind, that Schrempp was dangling hundreds of feet above the ground. And there was no guarantee that Messner would be able to stop his fall. The possibility existed that Schrempp would plunge to his death. Nevertheless, he jumped, and Messner did just as he promised. He stopped Schrempp's fall and lowered him gently to the safety of a ledge below.

Good leaders notice and reward the accomplishments of their team.

As Rick Pitino, coach of the Boston Celtics, says, ". . . when you're asking people to subordinate some of their individual goals for the sake of the group, you must let them know you are aware of their sacrifice. You must constantly thank them for it."

In my book *The Magic of Teamwork* I told about an inscription I read on a monument in Kansas City, Missouri, when I was speaking in that city on the Fourth of July in 1996. Because that inscription affected me so deeply, I'd like to take just a moment to retell that story.

The memorial stands in a small park at the corner of 40th Street and Main and is dedicated to the memory of Major Murray Davis, a Kansas City native who was killed in France during World War I.

I was out for an early-morning run when my attention was captured by the monument, so I jogged on over to take a closer look. Jogging in place in front of it, I read:

117

A KINDLY, JUST AND BELOVED
OFFICER, WISE IN COUNSEL,
RESOLUTE IN ACTION,
COURAGEOUS UNTO DEATH.

Intrigued, I ran around to the other side and read more about this brave man:

SERIOUSLY WOUNDED, HE
REFUSED TO RELINQUISH HIS
COMMAND UNTIL, MORTALLY
WOUNDED, HE FELL, LEADING HIS
COMRADES TO VICTORY. HIS LAST
WORDS WERE, "TAKE CARE OF MY
MEN."

That's all I know about the life of Murray Davis. But if the inscription on his memorial is accurate, I also know that he must have been one amazing leader. And, because of that, the men under his command must have made up one amazing team.

▲

People don't want to hear that I'm no better than my teammates. They want me to say, "I'm this or I'm that," but I'm not. Everything I am, I owe to this team.

SOCCER SUPERSTAR MIA HAMM

▼

It is never easy to be a good leader. It takes sacrifice and hard work. Thankfully, it rarely takes a sacrifice as great as the one Major Davis gave—his life. But a good leader does have to be willing to set aside his own desires and wants for the good of the team. As the greatest leader of all time, Jesus Christ, said, "Greater love has no one than this, that he lay down his life for his friends" (John 15:13).

3. Be Committed to Your Team

What do I mean when I say you need to be committed to your team? If you want to be successful, you must be:

▲ Committed to the other members of your team

▲ Committed to your team's purpose

▲ Committed to excellence

▲ Committed to winning

▲ Committed to continual improvement—in other words, be willing to practice, practice, practice

Mia Hamm is a young woman, who, I believe, demonstrates all of the above qualities. Under her leadership, the U.S. women's soccer team stunned the sports world by winning the World Cup in 1999. All the experts were startled by what the American women were able to accomplish. In fact everyone seemed surprised except Mia and her teammates.

And when the media tried to give Mia the lion's share of the glory, she refused it. She knew firsthand about all of the hard work that had gone into molding that collection of soccer players into a championship team. Those young women believed in each other, and it was that belief that allowed them to accomplish great things on the playing field. They had a common goal, a common purpose, a common commitment to excellence and winning—and it all culminated in a victory that made the entire country proud!

I believe that Mia Hamm's understanding of the necessity of teamwork was every bit as important to that American victory as was her tremendous soccer talent.

The year 1999 certainly had its ups. It also had its downs, one of these being the loss of one of the greatest men to ever play the game of basketball, a giant of a man—literally—named Wilt Chamberlain. Now I've had the privilege of seeing some great basketball players. I consider Shaquille O'Neal a friend, and I'm grateful for the many unforgettable moments he gave the Orlando Magic. What a dominating player! I've seen Kareem Abdul-Jabbar play, and Bill Russell—all the great ones. But for my money, the most dominating player to ever walk on a court was Wilt Chamberlain. I was in college when he scored one hundred points in a game for the Philadelphia Warriors, and if I live to be one hundred, I doubt that we will ever see anyone do it again.

But near the end of his professional career, Chamberlain came to the realization that one man scoring one hundred points was not the best way for a team to win a basketball game. In his autobiography, *Wilt*, he says he discovered that "it was essential to keep my teammates happy if I wanted my team to win. I not only began passing more and scoring less, I also made a point of singling my teammates out for praise . . . privately and publicly."

He found that such commitment to his teammates made each one of them try harder, "instead of maybe letting down, subconsciously, because he's tired of being ignored or hearing how great you are all the time."

No matter what team you are on in your life, if you want it to be successful and reach its goals, you must encourage teamwork.

4. Be Passionate about the Goals of Your Team

One of the greatest moments of my life was the night in 1989 when the Orlando Magic played their first game in the National Basketball Association. It was a great moment because it was the culmination of years of tireless effort on behalf of a huge team—consisting of hundreds of people—who were passionate— passionate about their city and passionate about their desire to bring professional basketball to their city.

▲

Enthusiasm is everything.

It must be as taut and

vibrating as

a guitar string.

SOCCER GREAT PELE

▼

Together we overcame obstacle after obstacle to bring the Magic into existence. If the people in the Orlando area hadn't been so passionate, the NBA never would have come to Central Florida. There were plenty of occasions prior to the awarding of the franchise when it looked as if we had run into a dead end. We could have collectively shrugged our shoulders, said, "Well, we tried," and walked away. But our passion wouldn't let us do that.

Of course, there's a lot of passion attached to sports. If you don't believe that, just tune in to watch the winners celebrate after the

Super Bowl, the World Series, or the NBA championship. You'll see a bunch of grown men jumping around like little boys, screaming and shouting and spraying each other with champagne. Why? Because they feel passionately about what they've just done. That's why someone said, "Sports is life with the volume turned up."

How many times have you heard a professional athlete announce his retirement by saying that the game "just isn't fun anymore"? What he means is that he's lost his passion.

Baseball's all-time hits leader, Pete Rose, said, "The first thing to go isn't the arm or legs. It's enthusiasm; it's passion. When that is gone, the player is through." Without passion, you're just going through the motions, and you're not likely to succeed.

Whenever I talk about passion, someone usually says to me, "But passion isn't something you create, is it? Either you have passion or you don't, right?" Wrong. Passion is an attitude about life. It's making up your mind, "I'm going to get excited about this!"

Unfortunately, in our society, passion about a job or a goal isn't perceived as being very "cool." It's more hip to be relaxed, detached, more than a bit cynical about everything. But such an attitude will not help to move you toward your goal, whatever your goal may be. Instead, try to do what business expert Tom Peters suggests: "Celebrate what you want to see more of."

If what you're doing bores you, then maybe it's time to do something else. If you don't really care whether your team wins or loses, then maybe it's time to reassess your goals and priorities.

But more often than not, passion starts with a decision to change your attitude. And it's a decision you have to make over again every day.

It's important to look for ways to nurture and feed your passion. It's just as important to surround yourself with others who are passionate about what you're trying to accomplish.

121

And, if you see your teammates' passion waning, it's important to put on your cheerleading outfit and do what you can do to rekindle their enthusiasm.

As leadership expert Warren Bennis has said, "All great teams . . . and all great organizations . . . are built around a shared dream or motivating purpose." Magician Harry Houdini asserted, "There is nothing more contagious than exuberance and enthusiasm, and it is sure to get an audience."

▲

> Without a doubt, our greatest strength on Everest in 1953 was our very strong team spirit. Individually, as mountaineers, we were not particularly expert people. We were competent climbers, but we worked together, and we were determined to get to the top.
>
> SIR EDMUND HILLARY

▼

I discovered very quickly, as I was heading toward the summit of Rainier, that there is no lack of passion on a mountain. Climbing that mountain was hard, hard work—by far the most difficult physical undertaking of my life. But it was also invigorating beyond belief. There was a feeling of joy that transcended the discomfort caused by the bitter cold and the aching muscles in my legs and back. Climbing a mountain—any mountain—is exciting!

When Sir Edmund Hillary was asked why he wanted to climb Mount Everest, he said, "Because it's there." He wasn't the first to give that answer. But I think that if he had taken the time to explain himself further, he would have admitted that it was passion that drew him to the mountain. If I were asked to give one characteristic of all the mountain-climbing men and women I have met, my answer would be "passion." They are, without exception, passionate about what they do. It is their passion as much as their skill that makes their achievements possible. And it is passion that calls them back again and again to ever more difficult challenges.

You may be looking at the mountains in your life and thinking, "If I can only conquer this one difficulty, then I won't worry about the rest." But the truth is that once you discover the excitement

122

and passion of defeating that first mountain, you'll be anxious to get started on the next one—and so on!

When someone asked former NFL Coach John Madden if he would ever consider retiring from his job as a television announcer, he said: "I'm never going to hang it up. . . . I'll just do it until they carry me out. I love the game. That's what I do. I couldn't live without it. I'm going to be a broadcaster forever!"

Wouldn't it be great to be that passionate about what you do? Just imagine what you could accomplish! A John Madden type of passion is what I want to strive for!

5. Think "We" instead of "I"

This one should be obvious. This is really what teamwork is all about.

Teamwork is the ability to work together toward a common vision.

It is the ability to direct individual accomplishment toward organized objectives. It is the fuel that allows uncommon people to attain common results. Simply put, it is less me and more we.

There are some things you don't want to try on your own. Climbing a mountain is one of them. Believe me, when the snow on Mount Rainier was coming down so hard that I couldn't see 10 feet in front of me, I was awfully thankful for that rope, which let me know that I was linked to team members ahead of me and behind me. Author Anne Zadra said, "The best thing to hold onto in life is each other," and when you're out there on a mountain, you discover just how true that is!

I remember sitting in a church service a few years ago and listening to a choir that just . . . well . . . to be honest, they were terrible. The reason they were terrible was that there was one voice that didn't fit in, even though it was a beautiful voice. The woman who owned the voice was obviously the most accomplished singer in the choir. But she wasn't singing as part of the team. She was louder—much louder—than the others. And the end result was not at all pleasing.

You see, on the most successful teams, there is a synchronicity. All the pieces mesh together into a cohesive whole. In baseball, the successful teams are not the ones that wait for a big blow—a home run—to win the game for them. Instead, the winning teams are the ones that do the little things right—constant hustle, laying down sacrifice bunts, practicing the fundamentals—these are the teams that demonstrate an attitude of "we" instead of "me."

I heard a story about an entrepreneur who wanted to build the best car in the world. So he took the engine from a Mercedes, the transmission from a Toyota, the rack-and-pinion steering from a Ford, and so on. By the time he was finished, he had a beautiful machine that included fifteen thousand of the best auto parts ever made. There was only one thing wrong. The car wouldn't start! The parts were great. But they didn't work together. Without teamwork, the whole thing was a failure.

When everything is meshing together as it should, there comes a sublime moment that transcends anything the individual members of the team could accomplish on their own. David Halberstam writes about this moment in *The Amateurs*: "When most oarsmen talk about their perfect moments in a boat, they refer not so much to winning a race as to the feel of the boat, all eight oars in the water together . . . the synchronization almost perfect. In moments like that, the boat seems to lift right out of the water. Oarsmen call that the moment of swing. Olympics contender, John Bigelow, loved that moment, but what he liked most about it was that it allowed you to trust the other men in the boat. A boat did not have swing unless everyone was putting out in exact measure. Because of that, and only because of that, there was the possibility of trust among oarsmen."

That moment of "swing" is what happens when all the members of your team are working together as one—when every member is pulling for every other member, and thoughts of "we" have become pre-eminent.

Before moving on to the next point, I want to make clear that I am not talking about setting aside your intelligence and letting the team think for you. That kind of cultish behavior is never beneficial. Nor am I talking about trying to copy the behavior of the other members of your team, like a teenager who has a hard time standing up to peer pressure. What I am talking about is this: When you are trying to achieve a specific goal—climbing a mountain, for instance—there must be a conscientious blending of skills and strengths, a setting aside of "what's good for me" in favor of "what's good for the team." There must be a willingness to set aside the desire for personal glory and concentrate instead on whatever it is the team is trying to accomplish. And let me tell you something. No matter how nice a person you may be, that last part isn't easy!

Tom, an acquaintance of mine, told me about the time he helped Jane, a friend of his, get a job at the firm where he worked. He wanted Jane to do well, of course. But he wasn't prepared for how well she did. It wasn't long before all the managers were coming around, slapping Tom on the back and saying things like, "Thanks for bringing Jane to our attention. She's a whiz!" Tom knew he should feel happy for Jane and proud that she was making an outstanding contribution to the company's goals. But he didn't feel happy or proud. He felt jealous. He tried hard not to feel that way but he couldn't seem to help it. And the worst part was that it was putting a strain on a friendship that went back nearly fifteen years.

You can probably guess what happened next. That's right, Jane was promoted over Tom. She didn't really want the promotion and seemed kind of embarrassed by it. She told Tom that their friendship was more important to her than any promotion, but he smiled and told her not to be silly and that he was really proud of her, even though he almost choked on the words.

But the fact was, Jane was very good at what she did, and the entire company was better because of her presence.

How would you feel if you were Tom? I believe most of us would find that type of situation more than a little difficult to handle. Tom eventually came to grips with Jane's success through lots of prayer and lots of positive self-talk. He came to see that the entire team—in this case, the company—was benefiting from Jane's hard work, and that meant that ultimately he too would benefit.

125

Because we have egos, it's usually not easy to get from "I" to "we." But if you want to be a success in life, it is absolutely necessary to make the trip!

6. Empower the Individual Members of Your Team

John W. Gardner, author and advisor to President John F. Kennedy, was always recognized as a brilliant leader, someone who got the most out of the people who worked for him. How did he do it? By giving his employees responsibilities that seemed to go beyond what they were capable of doing. He knew that if he wanted people to achieve great things, he had to empower them. He also understood that what business leader W. Alton Jones said is true: "The man who gets the most satisfactory results is not always the man with the most brilliant, single mind—but rather the man who can best coordinate the brains and talents of his associates."

Another man who understood the importance of empowering people was the late George Allen. Allen was a successful football coach for over twenty years—with the Rams, the Redskins, and finally in the United States Football League. In the fall of 1999, at a luncheon in Washington, D.C., I sat next to Bruce Keesling, who played for Allen in 1983 and '84, and he gave me new insight into Allen's success. Said Keesling: "George Allen had the ability to make you feel important no matter what your role was on the team. It didn't matter if you were the star quarterback or a wedge buster on the special teams. As a result, if you made a mistake on the field you felt as if you had let Coach Allen down."

▲

Treat employees like partners and they act like partners.

FRED T. ALLEN, BUSINESSMAN

▼

Despite the fact that there are some well-known and very successful coaches in this country who have the reputation of being screamers and yellers, I've never believed that belittling and threatening people is the best way to get the most out of a team. I prefer the approach taken by John D. Rockefeller, who said, "Employ-

126

ers and employees are partners, not enemies. In the long run, the success of each is dependent upon the success of the other."

When you share your power with the people on your team, you raise their enthusiasm and their level of energy. When they feel that they are partners with you, when they have a sense of ownership, they will expect more from themselves and they will work harder to achieve the goal. It's almost always true that when people feel empowered, they perform better. When they don't feel empowered, they're far more likely to be unmotivated.

Someone told me a story about a cruise ship that sailed into the middle of a terrible storm. The captain announced that his ship was in danger of sinking and asked for cooperation and teamwork to get everyone safely aboard lifeboats.

Everyone immediately pitched in to get the lifeboats ready, except for one passenger, who sat relaxing in his deck chair. Finally, someone came up, stuck an angry finger in his face, and demanded, "Why aren't you doing anything to help?"

"Why?" came the reply. "It's not *my ship!*"

Silly? Yes. But it illustrates the way people can react when they don't think they have a real stake in what's going on.

The attitude is likely to be: "The company's losing money? So what? It doesn't concern me. I'll just get another job if this one goes down the tubes." Or: "The team lost another game? I don't care. As long as I got my twenty points."

▲

Trust each other again and again. When the trust level gets high enough, people transcend apparent limits, discovering new and awesome abilities of which they were previously unaware.

DAVID ARMISTEAD,
EDUCATOR-AUTHOR

▼

Author Donald T. Phillips says, "The teamwork process involves many working members of an organization. As a result, when a final initiative is put in place, there are more supporters to champion the cause; more people to actually put the plan into action . . . which can be a major factor in overcoming an organization's natural resistance to change." He goes on to say that the old adage is true, "People support what they help create."

127

7. Build Trust and Respect

You're at an altitude of 11,000 feet. Snow is falling at the rate of 6 inches per hour. To your right, a sheer drop of 500 feet. To your left, a crevasse just waiting to swallow you if you make one false move. Tied to your waist is a length of rope that connects you to your teammates above and below you. In a situation like this, you had better trust the people you're with! And they'd better trust you right back.

I hadn't met any of the members of my team until I got to Mount Rainier, but during a difficult day of practice climbing, I came to know that I could count on their help if I got into difficulty on the mountain. And I think I showed them that they could count on me as well.

If you're trying to climb a mountain, you must have a team in place that you trust and respect. In fact if you're trying to accomplish just about anything in life, you need to have such a team in place.

There's only one way I know to build trust and respect and that's by showing other people you're worthy of it. When it comes to finding out who's worthy of your trust and respect, the best thing you can do is give it to people in small doses, and that will let you know if they deserve it in bigger doses. My attitude is that I trust people until they show me they don't deserve it. I've been disappointed a few times, yes, but surprisingly, not that many.

When the Chicago Bulls were kings of the NBA, they knew that their "go-to guy" was Michael Jordan. If the game came down to a last-second shot, Jordan's teammates were going to do everything they could to get him the ball. They trusted him. They respected him. They were happy to have the game's outcome in his talented hands. But he didn't get that kind of trust and respect overnight. He worked hard for it. It's going to be the same for you and me, but it will be well worth the effort.

In 1998 I was in my hometown of Wilmington, Delaware, promoting my book *The Magic of Teamwork*, when a man told me, "I work in an industry where teamwork is more vital than your business of sports, and I need to read your book."

"Really?" I asked. "What do you do?"

128

"I'm a brain surgeon," he said. "Usually, we have ten to twelve people in the operating room, and we may be in there for as long as twelve hours. The room is 'chapel quiet,' and we do everything as a team. No words spoken, except for requests like 'scalpel,' 'sponge,' and so on. We have to know each other and work together."

Can you imagine the trust and respect that is necessary in a situation like that? Teamwork can and does save lives!

And here's an even more incredible example of teamwork. Steve Hanamura, who was born blind, has run in several marathons. How does he do it? A bungee cord attaches him to his partner, Kit Sundling Hunt. Wow! Talk about trust!

8. Build and Model Character

Character is so important that it deserves more space than I can possibly give it here. That's why I'm devoting an entire chapter to the subject later on. But I do want to say that when it comes to character as demonstrated through selfless, goal-oriented teamwork, I have never been prouder of a group than I was of the Orlando Magic basketball team of 1999–2000.

▲

Character is doing what is right. Every day we have hundreds of choices to make. Character is getting it right most of the time.

FLORIDA GOVERNOR JEB BUSH

▼

They didn't win any championships. They didn't even make the play-offs, missing by one game and finishing 41–41 on the season. But if character and heart were all it took to win championships, they would have swept the NBA's championship series in four straight.

Lydia Hinshaw, writing in the *Daytona News-Journal*, said that the 1999–2000 Magic were "neither boring nor incompetent. They have not embarrassed us around the league, nor have they strewn their dirty laundry all over our community. They have not complained about our hospitality, or any perceived lack thereof. They have not pouted over who should be the 2-guard or quarreled over who should get playing time.

129

"They have not attempted to fire a coach. They have worked hard at their jobs, and pitched in around the community, too."

She added, "This Magic team has relied on teamwork and hard work," and said they were "a roster full of role models. Isn't there some way we can keep them all?"

What a group of personalities we had on this team! Tariq Abdul-Wahad, a native of France who spends his spare time visiting art museums; John Amaechi, an Englishman and a doctoral candidate in child psychology; and Michael Doleac and Pat Garrity, two young men who are using their careers in the NBA as a stepping-stone to medical school.

Not a Michael Jordan or a Shaquille O'Neal among them, perhaps. But I have rarely seen such teamwork and selflessness on the court. When the season started, the Magic were characterized as a group of rejects and castoffs. But they stayed in the play-off hunt until the next-to-last game of the season. Even in that game, an 85–83 loss to the Milwaukee Bucks, they showed their character. In the opening minutes, they couldn't seem to find the bucket and were quickly down 20–3. Instead of packing it in, they fought back to tie but lost when a three-pointer caromed off the rim as time was running out.

When it was all over, their disappointed coach, Doc Rivers, said, "I told them I was proud of them, and basically told them they're the best team I've ever seen, not the greatest, but the best." I felt exactly the same way!

Rivers went on to be named coach of the year in the NBA, beating out the Lakers' Phil Jackson by one vote. That says a great deal about the job Rivers did in molding the Magic into a team. After all, "Coach-of-the-Year" honors are almost always reserved for those whose teams are in the thick of a fight for the championship trophy.

Rivers was humble in his acceptance speech: "I've said all year that I felt I was the luckiest coach in the world because of the guys I had on the team," he said. "If I'm coach of the year, then I had players of the year and team of the year."

He added, "If I could explain our team in one word, it would be 'care.' They cared about playing. They cared about being coached. They cared about winning. They cared about improving. They cared about being teammates. And they made my job easy."

130

They typified what Chuck Swindoll says about teamwork: "Nobody is a whole orchestra. Each one is a musician. But take away one musician and the symphony is incomplete. . . . You guessed it! We need each other. You need someone and someone needs you. Isolated islands we're not. To make this thing called life work, we gotta lean and support. And relate and respond. And give and take. And confess and forgive. And reach out and embrace."

Let me close this chapter on teamwork with this statement made by John Hunt in his book *The Ascent of Everest:* "Comradeship . . . is forged among high mountains, through the difficulties and dangers to which they expose those who aspire to climb them, the need to combine their efforts to attain their goal, the thrills of a great adventure shared together."

Now as we've already seen, every team needs an effective leader. And that's what we're going to talk about next, in Life Lesson Number Five.

S·E·V·E·N

Life Lesson Number Five: Every Team Needs a Good Leader

The wise leader is not collecting a string of successes, but helping others to find their own success. Sharing success is very successful. It blesses everyone and diminishes no one.

The Tao of Leadership

No doubt about it. We're in a "leadership boom." Hardly a week goes by that I don't find an invitation to another leadership seminar in my mailbox.

There are dozens of books on the subject. Books about Lincoln on leadership, the Founding Fathers on leadership, Martin Luther King on leadership, Churchill on leadership, and on and on it goes.

I'm pretty sure that I've read just about every book that's been published on the subject of leadership—at least during the last ten years. And that was an awful lot of reading! The good news is that because I've read them all for you, you don't have to read them for yourself. I'm going to save you a thousand hours or so by giving you the *Reader's Digest* condensed version of everything—plus what I've learned through years of experience, as a leader and a follower. After all, I've followed a lot of leaders over the years, some good and some not so good. And I've learned from all of them.

I've also done my share of leading, and here too I have tried to learn through both my successes and my failures. Just about everyone finds that there are times in life when they are relegated to the role of follower. And when that happens to you, you had better be certain that the leader you're following is worthy of your trust.

There will be other times when the success of your endeavor depends on your stepping up to the front and assuming the role of leader. And when that situation occurs, it's important to lead effectively and with confidence. As mountain climber Stacy Allison says, "It's easy to become complacent and let others take the lead all the time. To really achieve our full potential, though, we must challenge ourselves." She asks, "How many good ideas never see the light of day because the capable people who conceptualize them don't believe they can convince others?"

The point is, you can't get to the top of the mountain without a good leader, whether that leader is you or somebody else. That's why in this chapter I'm going to talk about the most important qualities that go into developing an effective leader. My goal is to help you lead—or follow—in a way that will help you reach your destination, the summit of the mountain.

I am convinced there are seven qualities shared by all great leaders. They are:

1. Vision
2. Ability to communicate effectively
3. People skills
4. Character
5. Competence
6. Boldness
7. A servant's heart

I hate to think what might have happened to our little team trying to make it to the summit of Mount Rainier if we had not had an effective, caring leader in the person of George Dunn. There was never a moment when we did not feel confident in his ability to keep us together, moving toward our goal, even when the snow was coming down so fast we couldn't see more than 20 or 30 feet in front of us.

I don't know George Dunn very well, having spent only parts of two days with him on the mountain, but after only a few hours of working with him, I came to believe that he has all of the seven character qualities listed above. What I appreciated most about George was his ability to encourage us along the way, and believe me, there were times when we needed it.

When we got back to camp, I asked one of my fellow climbers, a woman named Gail, to give me her opinion of George. She said, "He's a world-class climber and could lord it over us and be a big shot, but he's one of us and really encourages us."

Let's take a closer look now at the seven qualities of an effective leader, beginning with vision.

▲

Vision is the essence of leadership. Knowing where you want to go requires three things: Having a clear vision, articulating it well, and getting your team enthusiastic about sharing it.

THEODORE HESBURGH,
PRESIDENT OF NOTRE DAME

▼

1. Vision

There were times on Mount Rainier when I wasn't sure I could put one foot in front of the other one more time. I was exhausted and disoriented by the glaring whiteness all around me. I had no idea which direction I ought to be going. All I could do was keep following where George Dunn was leading.

Thankfully, George never lost sight of our ultimate goal. He knew exactly where we were going and what we needed to do to get there. He was able to keep his eyes on the big picture. In other words, he had vision, a quality demonstrated by so many of history's great men.

135

As Jack Welch, CEO of General Electric, says, "Leaders . . . and you can take anyone from Roosevelt to Churchill to Reagan . . . inspire people with clear visions of how things can be done better."

When I consider men of vision, Abraham Lincoln comes quickly to mind. Following the North's victory at Gettysburg during the Civil War, the Union Army drove Robert E. Lee and his Confederate troops back into Virginia. At a meeting shortly after the battle, General George Meade told Lincoln that his troops had been successful in "driving every vestige of the invader from our soil."

The President was deeply offended by Meade's remarks. "Drive the invader from our soil?" he cried. "Is that all? Will our generals never get the idea? The whole country is our soil!"

Lincoln's vision went beyond the winning of a battle, or even a war. His desire was the healing and reunification of a country that had been torn apart.

In contrast, Jack Welch says that many so-called leaders of today "equate [managing] with sophistication, with sounding smarter than anyone else. They inspire no one. I dislike the traits that have come to be associated with 'managing' . . . controlling, stifling people, keeping them in the dark, wasting their time on trivia and reports; breathing down their necks. You can't manage self-confidence into people." Welch is right. Micromanagement stifles, rather than encourages, vision.

Welch has some very clear ideas regarding how effective leaders should operate. "First of all, they should be bursting with energy; second, they should be able to develop and implement a vision. . . . And, most important, they must know how to spread enthusiasm. . . ."

"Getting employees excited about their work," he says, "is the key to being a great business leader."

Mark McCormack asks, "If everyone started out as equals, how would the group's leader emerge?" Then he answers his own question, "In my opinion, you could tell the leader after a few minutes of discussion. He or she would be the one asking the most probing questions about the consequences of the group's decisions. He or she would be trying to anticipate the future."

The great nineteenth-century preacher Charles Haddon Spurgeon often told about a woman who asked artist Joseph Turner why he used such vivid colors in his paintings. "I never see anything like them in nature," she said.

Turner answered, "Don't you wish you did, Madam?"

In his imagination, he was able to see things the way he thought they ought to be, and his paintings were his means of bringing them to life. Albert Einstein understood this concept when he wrote, "Your imagination is the preview to life's coming attractions."

Former Senator Bill Bradley, a Rhodes Scholar and all-star for the New York Knicks, praises imagination because it "allows us to escape the predictable. Artists, scientists and poets use the power of imagination every day. . . . Above all, it enables us to see beyond the moment . . . to transcend our circumstances, however dire they may appear . . . and to reply to the common wisdom that says we cannot soar by saying: 'Just watch!'"

He adds, "When you inspire others to do the same, that's leadership. Leadership means getting people to think, believe, see, and do what they might not have without you."

Coach John Wooden elaborated on Bradley's words, when he said that a good leader must:

▲

You can have brilliant ideas, but if you can't get them across, your ideas won't get you anywhere.

LEE IACOCCA

▼

- ▲ Define the vision.
- ▲ Live the vision.
- ▲ Communicate the vision.

Leadership scholar Warren Bennis studied dozens of organizations, large and small, and discovered that the best of those organizations had leaders who "have developed a mental image of a possible and desirable future state of the organization. This image, which we call a vision, may be as vague as a dream, or as precise as a goal or a mission statement." He added that this "vision articulates a view of a realistic, credible, attractive future for the organization . . . a condition that is better in some important ways than what now exists. . . . Leadership is the capacity to translate vision into reality."

Vision involves knowing where you want to go, believing you have what it takes to reach that goal, and then charting a realistic path to get you there.

When the great sculptor begins his work, he sees much more than a shapeless lump of clay or stone. He sees instead the beautiful eagle or stallion that will exist when he is finished. You may feel right now that your life is shapeless or aimless, but with the right vision, you can see the beautiful thing your life can become.

As writer Robert Collier said, "Visualize this thing that you want. See it, feel it, believe in it. Make your mental blueprint and begin to build."

2. Ability to Communicate Effectively

Once again, there is nothing like being on a mountain, in the middle of a blinding snowstorm, to show you just how important effective communication really is. The members of my team and I couldn't just shout at each other. For one thing, the wind was blowing so hard, I could have yelled and hollered for all I was worth, and it's unlikely that anyone would have heard me. On the other hand, if I had managed to make myself heard, I was afraid that the vibrations from my shouting might have caused an avalanche that would have put all our lives in danger.

Heather MacDonald taught us how to "talk to each other" through such means as a simple tug on the rope that connected us all together. We learned to differentiate between a sharp jerk of the rope and a steady tug. We learned whether to tug once, twice, or three times. We also learned how to communicate by facial expressions and gestures—when the weather was good enough for us to see each other clearly.

We knew how important it was to pay attention to every signal George Dunn gave us. It was possible there would be hours when

138

he wouldn't have very much, or anything at all, to say to us. But when he did need to communicate, it was imperative that we were listening. Heather drove home the point that our lives could depend on our ability to communicate clearly, and we all took it very seriously.

It's clear to me that effective communication is essential for success in life—not only when you're climbing a mountain like Rainier. General Colin Powell understands the importance of clear, effective communication. He always told the officers serving under him to "speak up," even if they had something negative to say. "Bad news isn't wine," he said. "It doesn't improve with age."

General Powell also told his men that if he gave a command they didn't understand, "Ask me. If, after a second and third explanation, you still don't get it, there may be something wrong with my transmitter; not your receiver. I won't assume you are deaf and stupid."

Wouldn't it be great if there were more leaders like General Powell—men and women who wanted to make sure they got their message across, and who, when they didn't, wouldn't automatically assume that the fault was on the part of the listener?

Colin Powell's actions show that he understands several important keys of communication: He has an open-door policy; he understands that effective communication involves listening as well as talking; he understands that you have to communicate clearly, without the use of technical language or jargon whenever possible; he knows the importance of communicating directly to subordinates.

▲ *Have an open-door policy.* General Powell told his men, "If you ever leave my office and don't understand what I want, just march right in and ask me."

▲ *Listen as well as talk.* As Denver Broncos' coach Mike Shanahan said, "You don't learn from talking. You learn from listening. Last time I checked, I never said anything I didn't already know." He added, "When you listen to another person's concerns and suggestions, it alerts you to possibilities

139

that you might not have considered. Even bizarre ideas have something useful in them, if you just give them a chance."

▲ *Use technical language or jargon sparingly.* Author James O'Toole says, "The task of a leader is to communicate clearly and repeatedly the organization's vision, strategy, goals, and objectives, and to communicate its values, mission, purpose, and principles . . . all with the intent of helping every person involved understand what work needs to be done and why, and what part each individual plays in the overall effort."

▲ *Communicate directly to subordinates.* General Powell also knows that the effective leader strives to communicate directly to his or her subordinates, instead of passing information down a long chain-of-command that can cause things to become garbled and distorted.

In the words of Mike Armstrong, CEO of AT&T: "Communicate, communicate, communicate! You cannot be a remote image. You've got to be touched, felt, heard, and believed."

Along the same line of thinking, I really like what business executive Herb Kelleher says about communication: "There's a lot being said about the importance of communication, but it can't be rigid . . . it can't be formal. It has to proceed directly from the heart. It has to be spontaneous. 'Communicating' is not getting up and giving formal speeches. It's saying, 'Hey, Dave, how are you doing? Heard the wife's sick . . . is she okay?' That sort of thing."

When the people who are following you know that you really care about them, they will be much more inclined to hear what you have to say—and act on it.

In a survey undertaken by William M. Mercer, Inc., one-fourth of all workers interviewed said they were capable of doing at least 50 percent more work than they did. Taken altogether, the workers said they could do an average of one-fourth more work. Why didn't they? One of the main reasons was that they did not feel they were involved in decision making. In other words, when communication came, it was in the form of, "We're going to do so and so," instead of, "How would you feel if we did so and so?" You see, lack of communication can cause real problems in terms of lost production and lost dollars.

Gilberet Amelio, president and CEO of National Semiconductor Company, says, "If a leader can't get a message across clearly and motivate others to act on it, then having a message doesn't even matter."

Consider Ronald Reagan, who was often called the "Great Communicator," even by those who were on opposite sides of most political issues. Reagan always made it a point to communicate directly with his constituents. Even while handling the enormous pressures and responsibilities of the presidency, he reportedly spent some of almost every evening reading mail and writing out personal replies. No wonder Reagan will go down in history as one of the most popular presidents of the twentieth century. He said, "I've always believed that a lot of the troubles in the world would disappear if we were talking to each other, instead of about each other." He was absolutely right.

▲

Anyone who is a leader has to love his people. You have to make them feel they are an important part of your operation.

TOMMY LASORDA

▼

3. People Skills

Another thing about George Dunn. We all liked him. Did we like him because he was nice to us all the time or told us what we wanted to hear? No. There were times when he was tough with us. But he never belittled us or was condescending. When he had to get after us about something, we knew he had our best interests at heart and that he wanted to see us succeed.

What's more, his belief in us was contagious to the point where we also began to believe in ourselves. He believed we could climb the mountain and that made *us* believe it.

George Dunn had one of the most important qualities any leader can have. He had what I call "people skills." Leaders who want to get the most from their people can best succeed by showing them

141

that they genuinely care and want their people to share in all the successes and triumphs.

Some people protest that they just don't know how to do this. I've heard it said more than once: "You don't understand, I'm just not a people person." But having people skills doesn't have anything at all to do with your natural inclinations or your personality. It has more to do with what you do than with who you are.

▲ *A people person shows that he or she is willing to work as hard as everyone else, and right alongside them.* During World War I, when Douglas MacArthur was a colonel, he became known as someone who inspired the fierce loyalty of his troops. He was demanding, he was tough, and he expected his men to give him 100 percent at all times. But he also showed them that he was willing to share the danger and the hard work. He didn't just tell them what he expected of them. He showed them by his actions that he didn't ask them to do anything that he wasn't willing to do himself, and they responded.

▲ *A people person finds reasons to praise more often than he or she finds reasons to criticize.* John L. Beckley, founder of the Economics Press, Inc., says that some bosses "equate criticizing with leading, because it makes them feel important and puts the employee in a subordinate position, but that's not the way leadership works. In fact, it's often just the opposite. When you go all out to do an especially good job of something, is it because someone belittled you? Usually, it's because the person who asked you to do it took the trouble to tell you how important it was and how much he or she appreciated it."

▲ *A people person takes the time to get to know his or her people on a deeper level than "just business."* Former Phillies' manager Eddie Sawyer said that the key to his team's success on the baseball diamond came from the relationship he built with his players. "Knowledge of the game has to come second," he said, adding, "I felt that I couldn't know enough about a ballplayer, about his personality, his background. I would always make an effort to meet the players' wives and

142

parents. I wanted to know them. I think these things are important in the overall makeup of a ball club." Or any other kind of team.

▲ *A people person keeps the lines of communication open.* During World War II, General Dwight Eisenhower had a suggestion box outside his door. It was not there for decoration. He took it seriously and regularly reviewed each suggestion. German General Erwin Rommell had no suggestion box. Of course, that had no bearing on the Allies' eventual victory. Or did it?

▲ *A people person demonstrates integrity.* The truth isn't always pleasant. It's not always easy to tell. But people deserve to hear it. The leader who sugarcoats everything or who tells his people what he thinks they want to hear, is not going to inspire confidence. A friend told me he lost confidence in his supervisor when the man kept having what he called "pep rally" meetings to talk about how well everything was going for the company, even in the face of declining profits and the threat of layoffs. Absolute integrity in every situation is essential. If George Dunn had told us that climbing Mount Rainier was "going to be a snap," we would have decided after only about a hundred yards or so that we really didn't trust him.

▲ *A people person gives credit where credit is due.* Attorney Franklin J. Lundling says, "Any leader worth following gives credit easily where credit is due. He does not take someone's idea, dress it up and offer it as his own. He offers it as theirs . . . he plays fair with everyone and recognizes the strong points in people, as well as the weak ones."

Finally, if you are interested in being a people person, here are Dale Carnegie's six ways to make people like you:

▲ Become genuinely interested in other people.
▲ Smile.
▲ Remember that a person's name is, to that person, the sweetest and most important sound in any language.
▲ Be a good listener. Encourage others to talk about themselves.

▲ Talk in terms of the other person's interests.

▲ Make the other person feel important—and do it sincerely.

4. Character

To be a good leader, you must be a person of good, moral character. General Norman Schwarzkopf, in a speech at the University of Richmond in Virginia, said, "By far, the single most important ingredient of leadership is your character." He added, "You will find that 99 percent of all the leadership failures in this country in the past one hundred years were not failures in competence. They were failures in character."

Pete Rozelle, the former commissioner of the National Football League, once stated, "Character is what you are, and reputation is what people think you are. But if your reputation is bad, you might as well have bad character."

What does it mean to have character? It means that you:

▲ Strive to put the welfare of others ahead of your own interests.

▲ Always try to do what you say you're going to do, no matter how hard it may be.

▲ Are open and transparent in your dealings with others.

▲ Are honest, even when it doesn't seem to be in your best interest to tell the truth.

▲ Show respect to others, regardless of their station in life.

One of the best descriptions of character is the Bible's listing of the "fruit of the Spirit," as recorded in the fifth chapter of Galatians: love, joy, peace, patience, kindness, goodness, faithfulness, gentleness, and self-control.

Any man or woman who professes to follow Christ should demonstrate the character necessary to be a good leader. Unfortunately, we all know that's not always the case. It's too easy to cite examples of well-known Christian leaders who exhibited an utter lack of character. It's not my intention to point fingers. I certainly know from personal experience how frail human beings can be—

144

even the best of us! But I also think it's important to be reminded that character counts, especially in the lives of those who say they are followers of Christ.

For example, I heard that a survey of waiters and waitresses revealed that their least favorite day of the week is Sunday. Why? Because that's when the "church crowd" comes in and they don't tip very well. Someone says, "What does tipping have to do with character?" Only that a person of character, in addition to being honest and morally upright, would also be kind and generous to the best of his or her ability. Wouldn't it be great if the waiters had said that Sunday was their favorite day of the week, because the Christians were so easy to deal with—and were good tippers to boot!

I'm reminded of what happened when a group of pastors was staying at a hotel during a convention. Afterward, someone asked the hotel manager what sort of guests they were. "Well," he replied, "they didn't break any of the Ten Commandments. On the other hand, they didn't break any ten-dollar bills, either!"

I love what Peggy Noonan, speechwriter for Ronald Reagan, said about character: "A President doesn't have to be brilliant. He doesn't have to be clever. You can hire 'clever.' White Houses are always full of quick-witted people with ready advice on how to flip a Senator or implement a strategy, but you can't buy courage and decency. You can't rent a strong, moral sense. A President must bring these things with him." The same is true of any leader.

David Gergen, advisor to five United States Presidents, wrote, "A President of the United States must have more than informed judgment; he must also have the honesty, rootedness, warmth, and decency that make others trust him. Capacity counts, but once a candidate passes the test, character counts more."

▲

Leadership starts out with the whole issue of integrity and credibility. So, you have to be believed and believable. You have to be a person who honors his or her word . . . a person whom people can trust.

RAY STATA, ANALOG DEVICES CHAIRMAN

▼

Greg Morris, an expert on leadership, says, "Credibility isn't the result of a position or title. It isn't gained in a single seminar or workshop. Credibility is a pilgrimage, rather than an incident." And he adds, "Leadership is not measured by a wall of credentials or a list of impressive accomplishments. Touching people's lives is what leadership and ministry is all about."

5. Competence

We trusted that George Dunn could get us to the top of Mount Rainier because we knew he'd been there before—many times. In 365 trips to the summit, he had proven that he had the skills necessary to get us where we wanted to go. In his hundreds of trips up the mountain, we also knew that he had encountered just about every situation and every condition imaginable, and in each instance he had learned something new that he could impart to us when we needed it.

> ▲
> **Leaders can never take others farther than they have gone themselves, nor can they impart what they do not possess. You may not feel that you have extraordinary or spectacular gifts, but even the simplest things can be done with excellence.**
> LEADERSHIP EXPERT GREG MORRIS
> ▼

Blinding snow? He'd been there. Gaping crevasses? He'd seen them. Rock slides? He'd navigated his way around them on many occasions. Whatever was going to confront us on that mountain, we all felt sure that George would know how to handle it. In other words, he was competent. He promised he'd get us safely up the side of that mountain, and we all knew he'd deliver on that promise.

James O'Toole writes, "Effective leaders achieve their goals. For most leaders, that's all followers ask of them. Doubtless, the measure of effectiveness is, and must be, the least common denominator of leadership, for how could we call someone a leader who is manifestly ineffective? To be an effective leader is, by definition, to be competent."

146

I mentioned earlier that a good leader is willing to work right alongside his or her followers. A good leader also knows what he or she is doing and can teach others how to do it. There's only one way to get the kind of expertise and knowledge you need to be a good leader, and that is experience.

Maria Burton Nelson, who served as captain and leading scorer for Stanford University's top-ten women's basketball team, says she was twelve years old when she was first called on to be a leader. Several other girls gathered around her on a playground, urging her to play softball with them. She was surprised by their obvious desire to make her the leader because she didn't feel that she was any better at the game than they were.

She says it was at that moment that she thought, "If people are going to look up to me, I ought to become the sort of person who's worth looking up to." She worked hard, practiced hard, and did become the sort of person other people look up to, on and off the court. "That's how people become leaders," she says. "They practice."

And as they practice, they learn what works. They are not afraid to discard old ideas in favor of new and better ones. They agree with John F. Kennedy, who said, "Leadership and learning are indispensable to each other."

Once, one of Mahatma Gandhi's followers challenged him regarding his inconsistency. "How could you say one thing last week, and now say something completely different this week?" he asked. Ghandhi smiled and said, "Ah, because I have learned something in the last week."

As librarian John Cotton Dana said, "He who dares to teach must never cease to learn."

Admiral David Farragut, one of the Union's great heroes during the Civil War, was known as someone who sought constantly to learn new things. Another officer reported that Farragut once told him, "A Naval officer should always be adding to his knowledge. It might enable him to be more useful some day." Farragut is proof of historian Edward Gibbon's contention: "The winds and the waves are always on the side of the ablest navigators."

Now it's important to remember that it is not possible to be a competent leader in a hundred different areas—or even a dozen different areas. If you're looking to be a leader, lead in your area of expertise. If you're looking *for* a leader, look for one who has skills and knowledge in the proper area.

There are some areas where, frankly, I'd be one of the last people you'd want to lead you. If you're looking for someone to tell you how to play the guitar, for instance, I'm not your man. I have no competence in that area. But if you want to learn how to run the day-to-day operations of a sports business, then I'm the guy to see.

As Thomas J. Watson, founder of IBM, said, "I'm only smart in spots, but I stay around those spots."

6. Boldness

Writer Thomas Fuller said, "Boldness in business is the first, second and third thing." I'm not sure if he was right about that, but I do agree that one of the most important qualities of a successful leader is the courage to take action where others hesitate.

As author and former World Vision president Ted Engstrom says, "When all the facts are in, swift and clear decision is a mark of true leadership. Leaders will resist the temptation to procrastinate in reaching a decision, and they will not vacillate after it has been made." He adds, "There's only one way to know if you are a leader . . . and that's to step out and lead."

▲

Be bold. If you're going to make an error, make a doozy, and don't be afraid to hit the ball.

BILLIE JEAN KING

▼

James Burke, who eventually became CEO of Johnson & Johnson, was noted for his bold decisions. Early in his career at the company he would come to lead, one of those bold decisions nearly cost him his career. His mistake also cost the company a whopping $865,000 and brought Burke a summons to the office of General Johnson, the company's founder.

Burke was certain he was being called into the founder's presence to be fired and was shocked when Johnson congratulated him instead. The founder told him, "Nothing happens unless people are willing to make decisions, and you can't make decisions without making mistakes." He went on to tell Burke, "If you make the same mistake again, you're through, but that doesn't mean you should stop making mistakes." Thus reinforced in his determination to be bold and decisive, Burke went on to lead Johnson & Johnson through some of the most profitable times in the company's history.

What was true for James Burke is true for you too. If you want to be an effective leader, you must be willing to make bold decisions. And most of the time, your decision cannot wait until all the facts are in. As corporate executive David J. Mahoney Jr. said, "You'll never have all the information you need to make a decision. If you did, it would be a foregone conclusion, not a decision."

Danny Cox of Dynamic People Skills says, "In my study of achievers, I found that the difference between the great and the mediocre is one thing: the willingness to make a decision. If you think you've made a decision to build a great business and nothing is happening, then, you did not make a decision. You indulged in a fantasy, because action is inherent in any real decision."

During the Civil War, a staff officer questioned a decision made by Ulysses S. Grant, asking him whether he was sure it was the right one. "No, I am not," Grant replied, "but anything is better than indecision. We must decide. If I am wrong, we shall soon find it out and can do the other thing. But not to decide wastes both time and money and may ruin everything."

It's easy to find examples of bold, decisive leaders from politics, the military, sports, business, and other areas of life. But I believe that the boldest leader who ever lived didn't have anything to do with any of those things. You probably already know whom I am talking about. His name is Jesus.

As I read through the New Testament, I find that Jesus consistently presents a sterling example that any would-be leader would do very well to follow. Jesus consistently made difficult decisions and then he stuck with them no matter what. He never based his decisions on what other people thought. In fact he often did just the opposite, going against popular belief, against unjust laws and rules of his day, against the advice and wishes of friends and relatives, against popular wisdom.

He didn't base his decisions on what was easy. Instead, he based them on what was right, even though doing the right thing often got him into serious trouble and, in fact, eventually got him killed.

149

> ▲
>
> ... whoever wants to become great among you must be your servant, and whoever wants to be first must be slave of all.
>
> Jesus Christ
>
> ▼

(It's important to note that Jesus was doing more than just what was right. He was also "doing the will of my Father who sent me.")

Every time I read the life of Jesus, I'm amazed all over again by his courage. Often he found himself surrounded by people who were waiting for him to make one false step so they could pounce on him. Even so, he never shrank back from making the tough, and correct, decision!

Jesus acted boldly, and the entire world was changed forever because of it! Too often we have "leaders" who want their pollsters to tell them what the general public thinks about an issue before they are even willing to take a stand on it. "Give the people what they want," is not a good motto for a leader. It can only lead to disaster.

How wonderful it would be if we had more leaders the caliber of Harry Truman, who said, "I shall continue to do what I think is right, whether anybody likes it or not." Brian Mulroney, former prime minister of Canada, echoed that thought when he said, "Leadership means having the courage to make decisions not for easy headlines in ten days, but for a better country in ten years."

French statesman Léon Blum said, "I have often thought morality may perhaps consist solely in the courage of making a choice." Anyone who aspires to leadership must know that he or she will be expected to make bold choices and be ready to take responsibility for those choices. As Ronald Reagan said, "If God had given the Israelites a committee, instead of Moses, they'd still be in Egypt."

Leadership expert Tom Wheeler reminds us, "Successful leaders are the leaders willing to embrace risk." He adds, "Leadership requires the tenacity not to be undone by setbacks, coupled with the willingness to continue to take risks, despite the setbacks."

During the late 1980s and early '90s, the Detroit Pistons were the preeminent team in the National Basketball Association. But on one occasion, before the Pistons really began to jell as a team,

150

their coach, Chuck Daly, was becoming increasingly frustrated. They were loaded with talent, but their play was lackadaisical and their record was mediocre. Daly pulled his star player, Isiah Thomas, aside. "What is it you do best?" he demanded.

"Lead!" came the response.

"Well, then," Daly thundered, "get out there and lead!"

Challenged, Thomas did just that. It was no coincidence that the Pistons won the game that night, and lots of other games on lots of other nights!

7. A Servant's Heart

The thought has probably been expressed at least one hundred times, in one hundred different ways. The late Sam Rayburn, former speaker of the U.S. House of Representatives, put it this way: "You cannot be a leader and ask other people to follow you, unless you know how to follow too." The successful leader takes to heart each point of "The Follower's Creed":

> I will follow you, if you:
> Treat me with respect
> Inspire me with your vision
> Teach me
> Are tolerant of my mistakes
> Are visible and available
> Talk with (and listen to) me
> Allow me to grow
> Don't give up or change course arbitrarily
> Have the courage of your convictions
> Tell me the truth, and practice what you preach.

Jesus Christ told his followers that the leader among them must become "your servant." Then he showed them what he was talking about. In his final meal with his apostles, before his crucifixion, he wrapped a towel about himself and, taking on a task that was usually performed by the lowliest servant of all, took a basin and washed his followers' feet. As he did, he told them, "Now that

I, your Lord and Teacher, have washed your feet, you also should wash one another's feet" (John 13:14).

In Jesus' day everyone required constant foot-washing. People wore sandals, and it didn't take more than a few hundred yards on Palestine's dusty roads before a person's feet were filthy. Whenever visitors entered someone's home, one of the first acts of hospitality was to provide water—and a servant—to wash their feet. It was something that had to be done. But it was a task almost everyone felt they were too good to do. And yet Jesus did it.

Look around you. What do you see that needs to be done? Is it beneath you? Ask yourself if you would be willing to do it. If not, why not? And then try to picture Jesus kneeling down with that basin of water, like a "common cleaning man."

During the 1999/2000 season the Orlando Magic were in the middle of a close game against the Washington Wizards, and a damp spot on the floor started causing players to slip and slide around the hardwood.

The fans began to cheer when Wizards' player Juwan Howard got down on his hands and knees and began mopping up the wet spot with a ball boy's towel. It didn't matter to Howard that he was an NBA player with a multimillion-dollar contract. He simply saw what needed to be done and he did it.

Later, when asked why he had taken it on himself to mop up the wet spot, Howard replied, "I'm not bigger than this ballgame. I'm not bigger than a ball boy or girl. I'm an individual, just like they are, and if I can lend a hand in any way, that's what it's all about."

That is, indeed, what it's all about.

The actions of anyone who wants to be a real leader must show a readiness and willingness to serve others.

What does it mean to be a servant-leader? C. William Pollard, chairman of ServiceMaster says servant-leaders have these characteristics in common:

152

▲ They listen and learn from those they lead.

▲ They work at making themselves available.

▲ Their door is always open.

▲ They are out and about, talking and listening to people at all levels of the organization.

▲ They are willing to walk a mile in the other person's shoes.

▲ They become frantic learners and avoid the trap that so many so-called successful leaders experience . . . the "arrogance of ignorance."

Tom Osborne, who was in the running for the national championship nearly every year when he was head football coach at the University of Nebraska, says, "The essence of teamwork is servanthood. When players see the needs of others being as important as their own needs, they begin to reach out to those around them . . . as one player reaches out to another and demonstrates a willingness to sacrifice personal goals for team objectives, the attitude often spreads."

Osborne says he tried to model his coaching methods after the teachings of Christ, and that, as he did so, he discovered, "Life begins to have meaning and purpose when we choose to honor God and serve other people. He adds, "I tried both, honoring myself and honoring God, and life seemed to make more sense when I put God first."

Servant leaders are people who do not always insist that things be done their way but often get what they want because their followers appreciate the care and concern they show.

Ulysses S. Grant said that Abraham Lincoln "gained influence over men by making them feel it was a pleasure to serve him. He preferred yielding his own wish to gratify others rather than to insist upon having his own way." And yet, Grant also remembered Lincoln as someone who, in matters of public policy, always got what he wanted, but got it in the least offensive way possible.

Jesus said that anyone who wants to be the greatest of all must be the least of all. Milton Murray echoes Christ's words as he speaks of leadership today: "Servanthood is the fastest track to leadership," he said, adding, "Living to serve brings the greatest joy that humans can experience. Your leadership can make the difference. Become a servant, and you become a leader."

It is fitting to end this chapter on leadership with these words from Albert Schweitzer: "I don't know what your destiny will be, but one thing I know: The ones among you who will be really happy are those who have sought and found how to serve."

Life Lesson Number Four: Give Up the Right to Complain

Most of us are about as happy as we make up our minds to be.

ABRAHAM LINCOLN

If he feels sour, he shouldn't work here. We are selling happiness.

WALT DISNEY, ON ANY EMPLOYEE WHO HAD A NEGATIVE ATTITUDE

IT WAS BRIGHT AND SUNNY when we arrived at the base of Mount Rainier. You couldn't have asked for a better day for a mountain climb, or any kind of outing for that matter. It was the kind of day when you might want to stop halfway up the mountain, spread out a blanket, open up a picnic basket, and just take it easy for awhile.

In fact if you looked up at an angle of about 30 degrees, you could see a small knot of climbers making their way along the side of the mountain, and they were wearing short-sleeve shirts and shorts.

As the old song says, "What a difference a day makes." When it came my group's turn to attack the mountain, the picnic

155

weather of twenty-four hours earlier was long gone. Instead, we found ourselves heading into the teeth of a raging blizzard—in temperatures that hovered right around zero most of the day. To put it mildly, conditions were extremely unpleasant.

But we knew that a safe haven lay just ahead: Camp Muir was waiting for us, and we were all cheered by the thought of spending several hours in cozy comfort there. Some "comfort"! When we finally reached Camp Muir, we discovered that it had no electricity—or heat! No running water. There was nothing to eat and no hot coffee percolating in the kitchen. In fact there was no kitchen! There were just a few hard bunks if you were tired enough to lie down, and I certainly was.

So I lay there, eating my frozen Power Bar, listening to the wind howling outside, and I wondered how long it had been since I had experienced so much physical misery in one day. I couldn't remember. I finally decided I'd never gone through anything like it.

But I knew better than to complain. George Dunn told us several times before we started out, "There are no whine and cheese parties on the mountain." In case we'd missed that subtle bit of humor, he put it in even stronger language. "If you've got a problem—unless it's something really serious—I don't want to hear about it."

Looking back on it now, I can see why it was so important to make sure we all understood the "no whining" rule before we began our assault on the mountain. All it takes to ruin any type of venture is one complainer. He or she will cause other people to feel that conditions are worse than they imagined. They too will become whiners. And pretty soon the whole enterprise will collapse. If there had been a complainer among us, we probably would have turned around at about the 5,000-foot level and skedaddled back to base camp as fast as we could go.

All right . . . I do have a small confession. I did come close to whining at one point. When we were safely inside Camp Muir, listening to that angry, whistling wind, I sidled up to George Dunn and asked him in amazement, "Have you ever seen anything like this?"

His eyes opened wide, as if he'd just heard a hilarious one-liner, and a slight smirk played across his lips.

"Oh, yeah," he said. "In fact this is like a good day on Everest."

I discovered that Dunn had made four attempts on the world's tallest mountain. Once, he had made it all the way to the summit.

Now, even though it's true that none of the members of my little mountain-climbing group were complaining, I would be lying if I told you that we were all smiling and thanking God for our good fortune. We weren't!

But Dunn seemed to be having the time of his life. His attitude was positive, almost cheerful, the entire time. He seemed to relish every obstacle as a challenge to be overcome. Watching him made me think of Jean Baptiste Molière's statement, "The greater the obstacle, the more glory in overcoming it." Or, as former NFL coach Paul Brown said, "A winner never whines." In other words, attitude matters.

By the time I came back down from that mountain, I had a new understanding of just how much it matters. I wouldn't go so far as to call it a mountaintop revelation, but whatever it was, I suddenly saw, clearer than I had ever seen before, just how much a person's attitude can affect his or her entire life. To be more specific, I realized:

1. Having a good attitude can keep you moving forward no matter what obstacles stand in your way.
2. Thoughts and words have power, so choose them wisely.
3. If you're waiting for perfect, you're going to be waiting a long, long time.
4. A little bit of discomfort and disappointment can be very good for you.
5. There's a positive side to everything that happens to you.
6. Seeing things in a positive light can help you deal with adversity and turn setbacks into victories.

Let's take a closer look.

1. A Good Attitude Can Keep You Moving Forward

Having a good attitude can keep you moving forward, no matter what obstacles stand in your way. At a dinner in Orlando, I had the privilege of sitting next to a wonderful woman named Ethel—

a woman who perfectly fits the description of being "eighty-five years young." We talked of the places she'd been, the countries she'd seen. She seemed to have a boundless supply of energy and enthusiasm.

In the course of our conversation, I discovered that Ethel's husband, a doctor, had been killed in a private plane crash nearly thirty years earlier. Perhaps it was nosy, but I couldn't resist asking, "Ethel, did you ever consider getting married again?"

▲

The difference between a winner and a loser is, many times, a matter of inches. If you think you can do it, most of the time, you'll do it.

BASKETBALL GREAT
NANCY LIEBERMAN CLINE

▼

At that point her daughter, who was sitting on the other side of her, laughed and said, "Oh, no. No man could possibly keep up with Mom!"

"Well then," I asked, "have you done any dating?"

Her eyes lit up. "Oh, yes. Why, just the other day in the grocery store, a gentleman asked me if I wanted to split a dozen eggs with him, and I said I would. Later, when I came out of the store, he was waiting for me in the parking lot."

"Really?" I asked. "And what did he say?"

"Well," she answered, "he came up and asked me, 'Do you drive at night?'"

Our whole table erupted into good-natured laughter, and I'm sure most of us were thinking, "Maybe you'd better call this guy. Sounds like his attitude is a good match for yours!" Here was a man who wasn't about to let the fact that he could no longer drive at night prevent him from pursuing an attractive woman! He wasn't going to give up on the dating scene just because he was in his eighties! He was a wonderful example of positive thinking—which is so important to success in life.

Doctors are frequently accepting the fact that a patient's attitude has a great deal to do with how he or she responds to treatment. Dr. Bernie Siegel, an oncologist, is one of these doctors. He has written a number of books full of stories about patients who were longtime cancer survivors—despite the odds against them—primarily because they maintained a positive attitude. They received exactly the same treatment as other patients who died in a matter of months. But some of them survived for years, and many seem to have beaten cancer entirely. The only difference, Siegel says, was their attitude.

A few years ago, some scientists tried to find out whether attitude really has a direct effect on performance by carrying out an experiment involving some members of a major university's swimming team. They divided the swimmers into two groups and had them swim practice laps. The scientists told the first group that their times were truly amazing—approaching world-record status. Then they asked them to try again. During the second race, every swimmer's time improved.

By now, I know you're way ahead of me. You've already figured out what those scientists did with the second group, and you're exactly right. (And, yes, you're also right that it sounds kind of mean!) They shook their heads and told the athletes that their times were terrible and asked them to try again. Those swimmers' times actually decreased—significantly!

The experiment showed that a good attitude does more than make you feel better about what you're doing. It helps you do it better. The swimmers who were encouraged actually did better in their second effort. The swimmers who were discouraged did worse.

In another experiment, a group of elementary school students were told that a scientific study had proven that children with brown eyes were smarter than those who had blue eyes. Over the next few days, the brown-eyed kids began to do better in class, while their blue-eyed peers started to lose ground.

That was when an announcement was made that there had been a mistake. Actually, it was the blue-eyed kids who were smarter. Suddenly, things changed, and the blue-eyed children started to outperform their brown-eyed classmates. As author Nelson Boswell said, "The first and most important step toward success is the feeling that we can succeed."

During the Civil War, many of the Union generals were notorious complainers. George McClellan was chief among them. He never had enough supplies, enough troops, enough ammunition, enough anything. He constantly overestimated the strength of Confederate troops and, as a result, was slow to attack enemy positions.

U. S. Grant, on the other hand, rarely complained about anything. He rarely demanded reinforcements, complained about conditions, or quarreled with associates. Instead, he went ahead and led his troops to decisive wins in battle after battle with the resources he had in hand. It was his positive attitude, as much as his military expertise, that kept him moving toward ultimate victory.

In other words, McClellan was a pessimist; Grant was an optimist. Here are just a few of the ways optimists and pessimists differ, from the pen of writer William Arthur Ward:

The pessimist finds fault;
the optimist discovers a remedy.
The pessimist seeks sympathy;
the optimist spreads cheer.
The pessimist criticizes circumstances;
the optimist changes conditions.
The pessimist complains about the apple seeds;
the optimist plants them.
The pessimist imagines impending peril;
the optimist sees signs of prosperity.
The pessimist disparages;
the optimist encourages.
The pessimist creates loneliness;
the optimist finds friends.
The pessimist nibbles at the negative;
the optimist is nourished by the positive.
The pessimist builds barriers;
the optimist removes roadblocks.
The pessimist invents trouble;
the optimist enriches the environment.

I would add one more very important difference:

The pessimist stands still or retreats;
the optimist is always moving forward toward his goal.

160

Reginald Mansell put it this way: "A pessimist is one who makes difficulties of his opportunities. An optimist is one who makes opportunities of his difficulties."

It's not always easy to be an optimist. We live in a world that brings us plenty of disappointments, losses, and difficult days. It's easy to give in to negative ways of thinking. As one confirmed pessimist told me, "I always expect the worst, and then I'm never disappointed." Maybe that's true, but what a crummy way to live!

> *Positive thinking takes practice and discipline, but it's well worth the effort.*

As essayist William Hazlitt said, "If you think you can win, you can win. Faith is necessary to victory."

Television personality Oprah Winfrey asserts, "What we think is what manifests in reality for all of us. If all of us would only strive for excellence in our own backyards, we would bring that excellence to the rest of the world. Yes, we would."

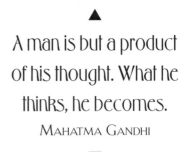

A man is but a product of his thought. What he thinks, he becomes.

MAHATMA GANDHI

2. Thoughts and Words Have Power

Thoughts and words have power, so use them wisely. Do you recall the story of *The Little Engine That Could?* Remember, as he made his way up the mountain, the Little Engine sang over and over again, "I think I can! I think I can! I think I can!" And then, as he gained strength, his song turned into, "I know I can! I know I can!"

Someone says, "Of course, I remember it. But why are you talking about a story that was written for children?" Because the story goes much deeper than that. Like many children's stories, it contains profound truths! It really is true that if you think you can do something, your chances of actually doing it improve dramatically.

If you think you can't do something, chances become greater that you will fail.

Positive thinking is essential for anyone who wants to get to the top of his or her mountain. And it's not only positive thoughts that are important, but positive words as well.

Don't put yourself down! Don't go around whining and complaining about how weak or inept you are, or that nothing ever seems to go right for you. Be kind to yourself. Expect good things to happen. Think and say positive things about yourself, and, just like that Little Engine That Could, you too will make it to the top of your mountain!

Author John Marks Templeton believes we must learn how to use our thoughts to assist us in creating the kind of life we'd like to have. He writes: "The human mind is a creative tool. We are either creating negative, limiting patterns that repeat themselves with deadening regularity, or we are creating new possibilities for positive expansion in our lives. Either we are creating doom and gloom or we are creating exciting possibilities. The choice is ours."

Mr. Templeton continues, "By turning our thoughts around, we can turn our own lives around. A consistent, positive attitude . . . allows us to turn an impossible situation into a positive opportunity to find happiness and success."

Dale Carnegie took that type of thinking a step further, saying that if we could learn how to consistently choose the right thoughts, we would all be "on the high road to solving all our problems." He said, "The most important lesson I have ever learned is the stupendous importance of what we think. If I knew what you think, I would know what you are, for your thoughts make you what you are."

In baseball you see it all the time. A hitter goes into a slump and loses confidence. He starts pressing, and that only makes the situation worse. Pretty soon, he's swinging at balls that are way outside the strike zone and he's thinking that he'll never get a base hit again. Usually all it takes is a couple of hits for him to get his confidence back. But some guys never get over it, and I've seen promising careers derailed by a lack of confidence and negative self-talk.

I was in a restaurant recently where the waitress was obviously having a very bad day. She was trying to give directions to a man at one of her tables but wasn't doing a very good job of it. She pointed to the east. "Well, you go down here about a mile . . . no, wait." She scratched her head and thought for a moment. "Go back up the street to the first stoplight. No, that's not it." Finally, she crossed her arms and shook her head. "I'm sorry," she said. "I'm not very good at giving directions." She sighed. "In fact I'm not good at much of anything." She turned apologetically and headed toward the kitchen with her head down.

Poor thing. She didn't know that, as educator Ralph Waldo Trine says, "Thoughts are forces . . . they have form, quality, substance and power." If that woman goes on complaining about herself, and believing that she's really "not good at much of anything," the power of her negative thoughts will hold her back in life, and she will never make it to the summit of her mountain.

Brian Tracy writes about the benefits one can derive from being an "inverse paranoid." He says "an inverse paranoid sees every situation as being heaven-sent, either to confer some benefit or teach some valuable lesson. . . . This form of inverse paranoia is the foundation of a positive mental attitude. This is the most outwardly identifiable quality of a high-performing man or woman. Your thoughts, vividly imagined and repeated, charged with emotion, become your reality. . . . Most of your self-limiting beliefs are not true at all. They are based on negative information that you have taken in and accepted as true. Once you have accepted it as true, your belief makes it a fact for you."

You can see why it's best to avoid negative thoughts and complaining altogether! That's the reason I try to take seriously the advice given by William M. Peck in the book *Worldwide Laws of Life*: "Your morning thought may determine your conduct for the day. Optimistic thoughts will make your day bright and productive, while pessimistic thinking will make it dull and wasteful. Face each day cheerfully, smilingly, and courageously, and it will naturally flow that your work will be a real pleasure and progress will be a delightful accomplishment."

3. Don't Wait for Perfect Conditions

If you're waiting for perfect conditions, you're going to be waiting a long, long time. During his ministry on earth, Jesus Christ often had a simple and direct request of the people he met. "Follow me," he said. And some did. But many more made excuses as to why that was not possible "right now." One man said he couldn't follow Christ because he had just gotten married and (understandably) wanted to stay with his wife. Another said that his father had just died, and (again understandably) he needed to stay home until he had taken care of all the arrangements and made sure his family was safely through this difficult time.

These people were waiting until the time was right to follow Jesus. They wanted perfect conditions. As a result, they missed out on the greatest adventure anyone could ever experience. There is an important lesson to be learned from this—the time to act is now. Not tomorrow. Not next week or next year. But right now!

We Americans are an especially difficult people to please. Here in Florida during the summer, we complain that it's too hot and we turn on our air conditioners. In the winter when it gets too cool, we fire up the furnace. Some cars even have dual climate controls so both people in the front seat can be comfortable! We have become used to having things just the way we want them and we complain when they don't work out that way.

▲

I believe in the sun, even when it doesn't shine.
I believe in music, even when I can't hear it.
I believe in love, even when I can't feel it.
And I believe in God, even when He is silent.

GRAFFITI WRITTEN ON A BOMB
SHELTER IN GERMANY
DURING WORLD WAR II

▼

164

But anyone who wants to climb a mountain has to stop complaining about the way things are and get moving!

Nolan Bushnell, founder of the Atari Company, said he believes that the most critical ingredient of success is "getting off your butt and doing something—it's as simple as that. A lot of people have ideas, but there are few who decide to do something about them, now! Not tomorrow. Not next week, but today. The true entrepreneur is a doer, not a dreamer."

For the last fourteen years of his life, the artist Pierre-Auguste Renoir suffered excruciating pain from arthritis. He was bent and twisted to the point where he was nearly paralyzed. Even so, he continued to paint.

During this time, Renoir's young friend Henri Matisse came to visit him every day. On one occasion, as Matisse watched Renoir painting, he could see that every brush stroke was causing tremendous pain. "Auguste," he finally said, "why do you continue to paint when you are in such agony?"

"The beauty remains," Renoir said, "the pain passes."

It was during this time, two years before he died, that Renoir finished one of his best-known masterpieces *The Bathers*. Had Renoir waited until the time was perfect to paint, the whole world would have been deprived of many of his exquisite works.

Actress Gwyneth Paltrow, who is noted for her boundless energy and optimism, said, "It's not as if you can shut out the pain of life, but if you face it head-on, with an open heart and mind, you can surmount anything."

In other words, if you've got the right attitude, conditions are *always optimum!* As Chuck Swindoll says, "Life is 10 percent what happens to us, and 90 percent how we respond to it. Attitude is the single most significant decision I make every day."

I'm sure it would be impossible to find conditions that were any farther from perfect than those that existed inside Nazi concentration camps during World War II. Viktor E. Frankl, who has written so eloquently of his life during that horrible experience, says: "We who lived in the concentration camps can remember the men who walked through the huts to comfort others, giving away their last piece of bread. They may have been few in number, but they offer sufficient proof that everything can be taken from a man but

165

one thing: The last of human freedoms . . . to choose one's attitude in any given set of circumstances . . . to choose one's own way."

Even in a grossly imperfect place like a concentration camp, conditions were right to show perfect love. You see, whoever you are, whatever your circumstances may be, *you can do something of tremendous importance*, and the time to do it is now!

4. Discomfort and Disappointment Can Be Very Good

Nearly forty years ago, Victor and Mildred Goertzel undertook a study of hundreds of famous men and women. They wanted to find out what had given these people the ability to accomplish great things in life. Was there one common thread that could be identified as a "producer of greatness"?

To their surprise, the researchers found that most of these people did have something in common. It was suffering. Out of 413 people studied, 392 of them had overcome very difficult circumstances to achieve their greatness. They also shared a common attitude. All had come to view their problems as opportunities, instead of obstacles.

I'm not surprised by this. It's just more proof of what we've known for a long time—that pain and discomfort can bring growth. "No pain, no gain," we say. And it's true.

> ▲
>
> When life knocks you to your knees . . . well, that's the best position to pray, isn't it?
>
> ETHEL BARRYMORE
>
> ▼

"The mother eagle teaches her little ones to fly by making their nest so uncomfortable they are forced to leave it. . . ." writes Hannah Whithall Smith. She goes on to say that God does the same thing to us. "He stirs up our comfortable nests, and pushes us over the edge of them, and we are forced to use our wings to save ourselves from fatal falling. Our wings are being developed."

I'm sure it's no fun for those eaglets when their mother is trying to force them out of the comfort they've known all their lives. Just as it's no fun for you and me when we go through difficult circumstances—like an uphill climb through waist-high snow-drifts in zero-degree weather! But when such circumstances do come along, as they will from time to time, we can react to them in one of two ways. Either we can let them stretch us and make us stronger, so we do everything within our power to overcome. Or we can become bitter, complaining people who give up and let difficulty defeat us.

Franklin Delano Roosevelt was thirty-nine years old when he was stricken with polio. Suddenly this athletic man who loved to swim, play tennis, and golf found himself in a wheelchair, a para-plegic. For the rest of his life, merely trying to stand up was a painful ordeal. But he did not let his misfortune turn him into a bitter, complaining man. Instead, historian Doris Kearns Goodwin writes, "the paralysis that crippled his body expanded his mind and his sensibilities." She says he seemed "less arrogant, less superficial, more focused, more complex, more interesting," and continues, "He had always taken great pleasure in people but, now, far more intensely than before, he reached out to know them; to pick up their emotions; to put himself in their shoes." In short, he devel-oped many of the qualities that led to his being elected president of the United States four consecutive times.

Rose Kennedy certainly knew her share of heartache and pain. When asked how she managed to stand strong despite all the losses she had suffered, she said, "Early in life, I decided I would not be overcome by events. My philosophy has been that, regardless of the circumstances, I shall not be vanquished, but will try to be happy." She says, "It is up to us to be cheerful . . . and to be strong, so that those who depend on us may draw strength from our example."

My friend Norm Sonju, former general manager of the Dallas Mavericks, tells me that an old San Francisco steamship company advertised that its ships were made with "wood only from the north side of the mountain." You see, that's where the bad storms were, and adversity makes for toughness. That company was saying that it used only the best wood.

University of South Carolina football coach Lou Holtz says, "I can honestly say, from the bottom of my heart, that I have never had a crisis in my life, or a setback, that's not made me stronger . . . if I reacted positively to it."

Charles Spurgeon said, "Many men owe the grandeur of their lives to their tremendous difficulties."

5. There's a Positive Side to Everything That Happens to You

In the last section, we talked about taking whatever happens to you—even if it's negative—and using it to your benefit. It's also important to realize that just about everything that happens to you has some intrinsic positive value. I am convinced that Romans 8:28 hits the nail squarely on the head when it tells us, "in all things God works for the good," in the lives of those who love him.

▲

I have often thought it would be a blessing if each human being were stricken blind and deaf for a few days during his early adult life. Darkness would make him more appreciative of sight; silence would teach him the joys of sound.

HELEN KELLER

▼

As Marc Roberts says in *Roberts Rules!*: "There's a positive side to everything that happens . . . it's up to you to find it and use it to your advantage."

In the 1920s Ernest Hemingway lost a suitcase containing all of his unpublished manuscripts. Remember, this was long before computers and copy machines. These manuscripts, which had been crafted over hundreds and hundreds of hours, had no duplicates. Naturally, Hemingway was devastated. He felt that the stories were lost forever. But his friend Ezra Pound did not see it that way. He felt that the loss could actually be seen in a positive light. Pound told his friend that when he rewrote the stories, he would remember only the best parts, and the weakest material would disappear from them.

Hemingway did rewrite the stories, and, as we all know, became one of the greatest figures in American literature. The stories were better the second time around!

Ivory Soap is the second–best-known brand name in the world, next to Coca-Cola. Just about everyone knows Ivory as "the soap that floats." And yet it was originally nothing more than a mistake, the result of a worker accidentally pumping extra air into soap vats at the Proctor & Gamble Company.

Alexander Graham Bell invented the telephone because he was trying to develop a hearing aid for his wife, who was nearly deaf. Several times he started to give up, but the thought of helping her drove him on. It was while he was working on the hearing device that he came up with the technology he later used to build the first telephone. Years ago Thomas Edison quipped, "I've made many mistakes in my career, and most of them ended up being patented."

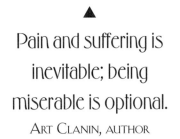

Pain and suffering is inevitable; being miserable is optional.

ART CLANIN, AUTHOR

About fifteen years ago *Time* magazine described a psychological study of several people who had lost their jobs three times due to plant closings. The psychologists who ran the study expected to find that these people would be beaten down and discouraged, but what they actually found was just the opposite. They came to the surprising conclusion that repeated adversity had become an advantage, rather than a disadvantage, in these people's lives. They had developed a more optimistic outlook on life, felt that things would always work out, and even had more confidence in their own abilities. A series of negative events had a cumulative positive effect!

My point? Don't complain when something bad comes your way. It may be the best thing that's ever happened to you!

6. You Can Turn Setbacks into Victories

Seeing things in a positive light can help you deal with adversity and turn setbacks into victories. In the Chinese language, entire words or phrases are often written out as one symbol. When two symbols are put together, the meaning may be quite different from what each conveys when written separately. Such is the case with the symbols for trouble and crisis. Standing alone, each represents something negative. But put them together and they combine to mean something positive: opportunity.

This is not a coincidence.

The Chinese language reminds us that times of trouble and crisis are actually opportunities for achievement and growth. It's all a matter of how we look at them and what we do with them.

As Pat Clarke, an Orlando television personality, writes: "Learn to accept your defeats with head up and eyes open . . . with the grace of an adult, not the grief of a child. You build your roads on today, because tomorrow's roads are too uncertain for plans. So plant your own garden and decorate your own soul, instead of waiting for someone to bring you flowers. Learn that you really can endure, that you really are strong, and you really do have worth."

In his book *Flow*, Mihaly Csikszentmihalyi says, "Many lives are disrupted by tragic accidents, and even the most fortunate are subjected to stresses of various kinds; yet, such blows do not necessarily diminish happiness. It is how people respond to stress that determines whether they will profit from the misfortune or be miserable."

There are several important reasons why adversity can provide you with an opportunity for growth:

▲ Adversity puts things in perspective. If you let it, it can help you focus on things that really count in your life. You can free yourself from trivialities and concentrate on what's really important.

▲ Adversity can make you stronger. As author Frederick Buechner said: "Even the saddest things can become, once we have made peace with them, a source of wisdom and strength for the journey that still lies ahead."

170

▲ Adversity can show you where you need to make changes in your life in order to prevent future difficulties.

▲ Going through a time of adversity gives you the ability to help and comfort others who may be dealing with the same situation.

▲ Overcoming adversity will boost your self-confidence and it will remind you that God is powerful and is at work in your life.

During the most difficult of his days at the forefront of the Civil Rights Movement, Martin Luther King demonstrated a remarkable ability to turn negative situations into positive ones. According to author Donald T. Phillips, Dr. King said: "I . . . realized that there were two ways that I could respond to my situation. Either to react with bitterness or seek to transform the suffering into a creative force. I decided to follow the latter course. Recognizing the necessity for suffering, I have tried to make of it a virtue. I have attempted to see my personal ordeals as an opportunity to transform myself."

In his book *Extraordinary Minds*, Howard Gardner calls this ability "framing." He says it is the ability to "construe experiences in a way that is positive, in a way that allows one to draw apt lessons and, thus, freshly energized to proceed with one's life."

Dr. King was one of those rare individuals who realize that the same boiling water that hardens the egg will soften the carrot—that everything depends on the individual's reaction to the stresses that are at work in his or her life.

In 1987 forest fires burned over 500,000 acres in northern California and southern Oregon. Once the fires were extinguished, firefighters were amazed to find thousands of ponderosa pine seedlings growing out of the ashes—baby trees that had, somehow, managed to survive without damage.

Before the fire, these seedlings would have had little chance of survival. They wouldn't have been able to get enough sunlight because it couldn't get through the tall trees that surrounded them. They most likely wouldn't have been able to get enough nutrition from the soil because, again, they were competing with the thousands of bigger, adult trees that grew all around them. But after the fire, they were able to flourish and grow. Here was proof that new life can, indeed, spring out of the ashes of death.

Are you going through a difficult time? Don't complain. Try to smile. After all, it may just be the beginning of a beautiful adventure!

And remember, no whining, no complaining allowed on Mount Rainier.

LIFE LESSON NUMBER THREE: DON'T GET CARELESS

When you feel how depressingly slowly you climb, it is well to remember that things take time.

PIET HEIN

Remember what the mama whale told the baby whale, "When you get to the top and start letting off steam, that's the time you're most apt to be harpooned."

BITS & PIECES

MADE IT TO THE TOP of your mountain? Congratulations! You're halfway to your goal!

Someone says, "What do you mean, 'halfway'? If I'm standing on top of the mountain, that means I've reached my goal, doesn't it?"

Not exactly. You still have to get back home. And in mountain climbing, most accidents do not happen on the way up the mountain but on the way down! There are a couple of reasons why this is so. They are called "yesterday" and "tomorrow."

In other words, climbers are so busy thinking about what happened yesterday or what's going to happen tomorrow that they forget to pay careful attention to what's going on right now! For example, a climber may be thinking about that wonderful moment when he or she first set foot on the summit—reliving the glory of yesterday.

Or the climber may be thinking about the delicious dinner and comfortable bed that are waiting back at the base of the mountain, or how he or she is going to be the toast of the town back home, telling everyone about the successful climb all the way to the summit.

Either way, the climber has lost focus. The climber ought to be going back down the mountain the same way he or she made it to the top—rest-stepping and pressure-breathing all the way. But the person has become careless, and that's an invitation for tragedy to strike.

As mountain climber Stacy Allison says: "When you get to the top, you've only done 50 percent of the work. You have to get back down. Some people . . . and organizations . . . spend all their energy, resources and vision getting to the top, but the top is the most vulnerable place to be. We cannot survive on top of our mountains." Another veteran climber, John Roskelley, put it even more concisely when he said, "You've got to know when to turn around."

In our increasingly mobile society, the National Safety Council reminds us that most serious automobile accidents still happen within a few miles of home. I suspect this is due to the fact that the drivers involved are at ease, completely comfortable with their surroundings, and, thus, careless. It's amazing what a moment of inattention can do. I just read a newspaper story about a serious automobile accident that was apparently caused when a woman looked down to change the radio station in her car.

Don't think you can relax your attention for a moment. You can't. You must stay alert and focused if you want to scale the mountains in your life.

Mountaineer David Breashears refers to this when he says, "The finish line of Everest is not the top; it's on the bottom. Reaching the summit is a moment when I focus and start to turn home. At the top of Everest, I'm in survival mode. All the exhilaration and

174

rewards of reaching the summit come later, in safety. I've been on Everest with unforgiving winds. There's no room for mistakes. The wind will freeze your skin."

Bill Crouse says, "The summit of Everest is pretty amazing, but all the way up, I know summiting is optional; coming home is mandatory."

Over and over again, veteran climbers warn of the dangers that come from letting your guard down for even a moment on the mountain. Here's what just a few of them have to say:

Alan Hobson: *"It is ironic, but true, that you can be in the greatest danger just when you think you're safe in the mountains. On Everest, especially, you cannot afford to let your guard down, even for a second."*

Rob Hall: *"With enough determination, any bloody idiot can get up this hill (Everest). The trick is to get back down alive."* (In May of 1996 Rob lost his life on the way down from the summit of Everest.)

Ruth Anne Kocour: *"Forget where you are and let down your guard, even for a minute, and the mountain may claim you forever."*

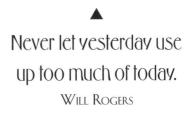

Never let yesterday use up too much of today.

WILL ROGERS

Jim Whittaker: *"The most dangerous part of climbing is coming down; not going up."*

Sir Edmund Hillary: *"You know, to mountaineers, it's one thing getting to the top, but it's another getting back to the bottom."*

Beck Weathers: *"One of the things that you must honestly ask yourself on a mountain—it is a moral obligation to your fellow climbers—is, 'With this step, how much do I have left? Can I still turn around and get back down to safety?'"*

All of this is more than just talk. There are statistics to back it up. One out of every twenty-nine climbers who make it to the top of Everest loses his or her life on the way back down.

I wonder how many of those people died because they quit paying attention for just an instant—because they were lost in yesterday or tomorrow instead of paying attention to today. In the pages ahead, I want to talk about how today you can use the lessons and experiences of the past to build a bright future.

Three Important Things to Remember about Yesterday

1. *Yesterday may be a nice place to visit, but you shouldn't try to live there.* You couldn't really blame singer Tom Jones if he spent a lot of time thinking about the 1960s and '70s, when he was one of the hottest acts around. During those years, he churned out one million-selling record after another. He sold out concert halls throughout the world. Women screamed—and sometimes fainted—whenever he sang.

Yes, indeed, those years were very kind to Tom Jones. But he still doesn't want to live there. "You can't live in the past," he says. "A lot of people who I started with in the 1960s are still there. I want to compete with what's out there today. I want to keep fresh."

Hall of Fame pitcher Steve Carlton feels the same way: "I try not to look back." He says of the past, "It's nowhere; it doesn't exist anymore."

Former Miami Dolphins' football coach Don Shula always gave his players twenty-four hours to savor a victory. During that time, they could relive the glory all they wanted to. But after that, it was time to let it go and start preparing for next week's opponent. He knew that past success had very little to do with what was going to happen in the future. He didn't want his players to be caught flat-footed, looking back when they should have been paying careful attention to right now. He agreed with Casey Stengel, who said, "Last year is past history. Never look back. Go back out and beat 'em again this year."

Of course, nostalgia can be fun. That's why, in the 1970s, there was a hit TV show about the '50s called *Happy Days*. And it's the reason there's a show today called *That 70s Show*. In another ten or fifteen years, there's certain to be a hit program called *Those Zany Nineties*, or perhaps, *Those Wacky Oughts*.

It's easy to have a selective memory about the past, remembering only the good and forgetting the bad. We look back on the fifties as a time of greasy hair, rock 'n' roll, hula hoops, and little more—forgetting the constant fear of nuclear war that hung over this country at the time, and the racial injustice that was prevalent throughout much of the United States. We think of the seventies as that crazy era of disco music and leisure suits—preferring

176

not to think about the Watergate scandal that brought down a president or the mass starvation that took place in places like Biafra and Bangladesh.

Some people like to stay in the past because it's secure. They already know what happened back there—as opposed to the future, when anything can occur. But you can't live in the past. If you try, it prevents you from doing anything constructive today to build a better tomorrow for yourself and your family. Every era—and every period of a person's life—has its fun times, its craziness, its triumphs, and its celebrations. But every era also has its tragedies, its serious moments, and its times of loss and mourning.

Theater critic Brooks Atkinson said, "In every age, 'the good old days' were a myth. No one ever thought they were good at the time. For every age has consisted of crises that seemed intolerable to the people who lived through them."

In his book *Stolen Seasons*, David Lamb writes, "Nostalgia is a dangerous obsession. It turns stumblebums into princes and dunghills into shining mountain peaks. It makes yesterday sweeter than tomorrow can ever be."

2. *Let the past go, but hang on to the things it taught you.*

Some people can't let go of the past for a different reason. They experienced some failure, tragedy, or setback that has become the defining moment in their lives.

Dr. James Dobson of *Focus on the Family*, says, "If I were to draw a caricature, I would depict a bowed, weary traveler. Over his shoulder, I would place the end of a mile-long chain, to which is attached tons of scrap iron, old tires and garbage of all kinds. Each piece of junk is inscribed with the details of some humiliation: a failure, an embarrassment, a rejection from the past. He could let go of the chain and free himself from the heavy load which immobilizes and exhausts him, but he is somehow convinced that it must be dragged throughout his life."

Author-poet Malcolm Boyd says the same thing in a much different way: "Letting go of an agonizing, unresolved problem rooted in the past can be essential to our ability to concentrate on living as fully as possible in the present. Our sanity and well-being require us to stop being obsessed by past events or misunderstandings that threaten to destroy our present happiness."

Boyd reminds us of the apostle Paul's words from the third chapter of Philippians. "Forgetting what is behind and straining toward what is ahead, I press on" (vv. 13–14).

Yes, it is important to be able to relinquish the events of the past to the degree that we are no longer bound by them. But at the same time, as George Santayana said, "Those who cannot remember the past are condemned to repeat it."

I think of "good old Charlie Brown," who always seemed to forget that Lucy would never really let him kick that football. How many times did she play that cruel trick on him? Dozens, at least. Sometimes I'd pick up the Sunday comics and want to shout at him, "Don't do it, Charlie Brown! She's going to pull it away at the last moment, and you'll wind up flat on your back!" But he never seemed to learn from past mistakes.

> *It's important not to let the mistakes you've made in the past keep you in bondage. It is also important to learn from your mistakes so you don't repeat them.*

On the mountain I made the mistake of getting confused in the blinding snow and separating myself from the rest of the group. Of course, I was embarrassed by what had happened, especially when George Dunn told me in no uncertain terms what a dangerous thing I had done. My very life was at stake. On the mountain, I didn't have time to brood about it or nurse hurt feelings. I knew he was right. And I'll tell you something else I didn't do: I didn't make the same mistake again. I learned from it and let it help me. I believe that if you can learn something important from a mistake you've made, then that mistake may be one of the best things you've ever done! Remember your mistakes so you can learn from them but do not let them hold you back. As educator L. Thomas Holdcroft said, "The past is a guidepost, not a hitching post."

I think it's also important to remember the times other people helped you in some way, showed you mercy when you were in trouble, or forgave you when you needed it. Remembering those occasions will cause you to be more willing to help others, show them mercy, and forgive them when they have wronged you in some way.

Bill Bradley says that when he first began playing professional basketball for the New York Knicks, he agonized over every mistake he made on the basketball court and replayed every loss over and over again in his mind. Then, midway through his second season, he made a bad pass near the end of a game that resulted in a Knicks' defeat. Bradley was beside himself until teammate Dave DeBusschere told him, "Sure you blew it tonight, but when it's over, it's over. Let it go. Otherwise, you won't be ready to play tomorrow night."

Bradley says, "That advice helped. I realized that the more you carry the past around, the less likely it is that the future will improve." He resolved that the next time he found himself in a similar situation, he would make sure his pass was on target. He would learn from the careless error that had cost his team a defeat, but he would not allow himself to be bound by it.

Test pilot Chuck Yeager once said, "The only time you want to look back is when you want to learn something," and I think that is absolutely true. Best-selling author and motivational speaker Zig Ziglar put it this way: "Make friends with your past so you can focus on today, which will make your tomorrows even better."

Sometimes, the only way you can "make friends" with the past is to confront it head-on. If you made mistakes or decisions that hurt other people, you may need to seek forgiveness. If you made decisions that have hurt you personally, you may need to try to undo them.

Christian psychologist Stephen Arterburn says in *The Power Book*, "It is so much easier to walk away from a hurtful past than to confront the issues, but we cannot remove the past from our hearts . . . it is there to stay. The only hope for true peace with the past is to face it at its worst; to seek to forgive, to be forgiven, to make amends, and to be reconciled."

3. *You can't change what happened yesterday no matter how hard you try, so don't spend time worrying about it!*

Which two words would you consider to be the saddest in the English language? For my money, they are "if only." "If only I had done this." "If only this hadn't happened," "If only I was a little bit smarter . . . or taller . . . or better looking," and on and on.

My son Bobby isn't what you'd call tall. He's 5'7". He was a good baseball player. He did well in both high school and college, and I couldn't be more proud of him. As I write this, he's in graduate school and also coaching in the Cincinnati Reds organization. It's not just fatherly pride talking when I tell you that Bobby has an excellent career ahead in baseball as a coach or manager. But I can't begin to tell you how many times I've heard him say that he wishes he were taller. One time he told me, "I think about it every day."

What I tell my son is the same thing I would tell everybody else. Get rid of "if only" thinking! You can achieve excellence *as you are!*

"If only." Those two little words have certainly caused a great deal of pain and suffering. One psychiatrist reported that the most success he had ever had in helping his patients was when he taught them to substitute the words "next time" for "if only." He said, "Many of my patients have spent their lives living in the past, anguishing about what they should have done in various situations. 'If only I had prepared better for that interview. . . .' 'If only I had expressed my true feelings to the boss. . . .' 'If only I had taken that accounting course. . . .'"

He helped his patients "stop wallowing in a sea of regret," and advised them to "tell yourself, 'Next time I am going to be prepared. . . .' 'Next time, I am going to speak out. . . .' 'Next time I have a chance, I am going to take that class. . . .' And so on."

He said, "Practice this simple technique until it becomes a habit. Never rehash errors you have made." And he advised his patients to "devote your thoughts to the present and the future instead of the past."

In her book *Your Intelligent Heart*, Susan B. Wilson says that thinking about what might have been, or could have been "if only" something or other had happened, is "hopeless meandering, [that] steals your time and energy." She adds, "If you feel the need to worry or live in the past, do so for a specific amount of time each week, and then STOP. Redirect your precious time and energy to actions that help you make progress toward your goals."

Television personality Pat O'Brien says, "The thing to learn from winners is how to move on. Great athletes have incredible capacity to forget their mistakes. So, learn from your mistakes, but don't dwell on them." He cites Michael Jordan who, during the height of his career, could "miss seven shots in a row and not hesitate a moment to shoot the eighth. He says to himself, 'I know I'm not terrible. I just have to keep shooting until I hit one.'"

Chuck Swindoll says there isn't a person alive who "doesn't have a store of painful memories." Then he adds, "We do not need to be defeated by bad memories."

Three Important Things to Remember about Today

1. *Always make the most of your time.*

The story is told that when Benjamin Franklin was a young man, a potential customer came to his print shop and asked how much it would cost to have some flyers printed. The man didn't like the price Franklin quoted him and began to argue. He pointed out that the flyers were small and didn't have that much type on them, and he asked Franklin to reconsider. Without batting an eye, Franklin said, "All right," and quoted the man a price that was substantially higher than the first estimate!

Of course, the fellow was astounded, more than a little offended, and continued to argue. Only this time Franklin's price went up even more. Exasperated, the would-be customer asked what was going on. Franklin reportedly replied, "You have been taking up my time by continuing to argue with me, and time is precious." Thus the cost of the job went up, not down.

I have no idea if that really happened or if it's merely one of those "young George versus the cherry tree" type stories, but it sounds like Franklin, and it makes a good point: Time is valuable. Time should not be

▲

You carefully count and check your dollars, but do you count and check, with equal seriousness, that indispensable possession that is so necessary for the acquisition of dollars . . . time?

THOMAS J. WATSON SR.,
BUSINESSMAN

▼

181

squandered or taken lightly. As Franklin himself said, "Dost thou love life? Then do not squander time, for that's the stuff life is made of."

Suppose you won a lottery in which you would be given $86,400 every morning. But then, by the same time the next day, whatever part of the money you hadn't spent would be taken away from you. Would you make sure you spent every dime of that money?" I'm sure you'd try. Well, the truth is that every morning, you are given 86,400 seconds to use as you will during the next 24 hours.

> *Far too many of us don't treat time as if it is a precious commodity. Instead, we go around "killing it," until it eventually kills us.*

Dr. Billy Graham spoke to this when he wrote: "You possess a nonrenewable resource, which is headed toward total depletion, and that resource is time. You can either invest your life or let it dribble through your fingers like time in an hour glass. If there is ever a time to redeem every second, every minute, it is now. You may never have tomorrow. You can't count your days, but with the Lord as your Savior, you can make your days count."

Stanley Marcus, of Neiman-Marcus, said he believed the one thing high-achieving people have in common is that they do not waste time. He said, "Time is probably the most precious asset I have, and which I have in the least supply." He added that he had to closely guard his time because, "The world has expanded in almost all directions, but we still have a twenty-four-hour day."

Time-management experts have figured out that in the average person's lifetime, he or she will spend:

7 years in the bathroom
6 years eating
5 years waiting in line
4 years cleaning the house

3 years in meetings
1 year looking for things that have been misplaced
8 months reading junk mail
6 months sitting at red lights
5 days brushing your teeth

Sadly, the same time-management experts have found that the average person spends about four minutes per day conversing with his or her spouse and thirty seconds in conversation with his or her children. This means, if you are average in these categories and you live to be seventy years old, you will have spent seventy-one days talking to your spouse, and just under nine days conversing with your kids. How can you change these unfortunate numbers? By planning ahead and resolving to make better use of your time.

Rob Gilbert, editor of *Bits & Pieces*, reports on a college professor who interviewed hundreds of highly productive people to find out how they spent their days. From their answers to his questions, he came up with a plan to make each day as productive as possible. He said that highly productive people:

▲ Prioritize and plan their work for the day.
▲ Make a firm commitment to stick to their plan for the day, no matter what.
▲ Get down to business as soon as they get to work.
▲ Enjoy what they're doing and feel that being productive increases their energy.
▲ Continue to work even when enjoyment fades or frustration sets in, rising above their feelings to keep their commitments.
▲ Complete their projects.
▲ Find joy in being able to say, "I'm glad I did," instead of "I wish I had."

In his book *From Everest to Enlightenment*, Alan Hobson says, "If I could take one thing forward from my Everest experiences, it would be the Sherpas' ability to live in the present, to understand that each moment is a present and that we are given it, in fact, *gifted it*."

Sometimes, it takes a near tragedy to help us understand time's importance. In *A View from the Ridge*, best-selling author Morris West writes: "Ask anyone who has survived a cardiac event, and they will tell you the same thing: every hour of every day is a bonus. You prize people. You understand that they can be as fragile and fearful as you have been. You don't quarrel any more; you discuss. You don't grasp at things, because, after all, the Creator didn't close His hand on you, but let you sit, quietly, like a butterfly on His palm."

Speaker Steve Sobel says, "I have learned, from speaking to many cancer survivor groups, that the watch on your hand no longer says, 'tick, tick, tick.' It now says 'precious, precious, precious.' When you understand that, every chapter in your life that you write becomes fascinating."

Let's agree right now that it will not take a serious illness or some other tragedy to make us realize exactly how precious time can be!

2. The best time to do anything is today!

In late May 2000 I drove from Orlando to Atlanta to cheer for the Georgia Southern University baseball team. My son Bobby, twenty-three, is an assistant coach there, and his team was playing in the NCAA tournament, trying to qualify for the College World Series. Unfortunately they were eliminated by tough back-to-back losses to Georgia Tech and Auburn.

After the second game, I congratulated Bobby for his successful season and, despite his disappointment, we talked with some anticipation about his upcoming summer job, coaching for the Cincinnati Reds' minor league team in Billings, Montana.

Finally, the time came to leave, so I gave him a hug, got back in my car, and drove off in the direction of Orlando. Suddenly, a sense of sorrow and heaviness enveloped me. At first, I couldn't figure out where it came from. And then it hit me.

My father and I had had a very similar conversation, almost thirty-eight years to the day previously. It was my senior year in college and my Wake Forest baseball team had just been eliminated from the NCAA tournament in Gastonia, North Carolina, by Florida State. After the game, my dad and I talked about my chances for a career in pro ball. Then we said our good-byes. I got on the team bus to go back to school, and he got in his car to drive back home to Wilmington, Delaware.

Dad never made it home. During the middle of the night, between Washington and Baltimore, his car went out of control, smashed into a bridge abutment, and he was killed instantly. Tears stung my eyes as I thought about my dad and how much it hurt me to lose him. And I wished I had hugged Bobby a little bit tighter and told him just one more time how proud he makes me and how much I love him.

Please, if you have something to say to someone, say it now. Let that person know you love him or her while you still have the time! Don't delay. Hall of Fame quarterback Bob Griese said, "One thing is really true: We had better use and enjoy the time we've got while we've got it. We assume we're going to live to be seventy or eighty years old—but there are no guarantees in life." He goes on to advise us to make every day count and to appreciate all that God has given us to enjoy.

I think of a friend of mine who has a whole bunch of really terrific ideas. But he never does anything with them. He writes them down, puts them in his briefcase, and plans to get around to putting them into action someday. But if someday ever comes around, somebody's going to have to give me CPR, because I know I'll have a heart attack!

Every New Year's Day, this fellow makes a resolution that "this is going to be the year" when he finally starts turning those dreams into reality. But for some reason, he just cannot seem to get off the starting block. Whenever I think about this friend, the words of psychologist William James come to mind: "If you want to make an easy job harder, just keep putting it off. Nothing is so fatiguing as the eternal hanging on of an uncompleted task."

Or, as that great philosopher Art Buchwald put it: "Whether it's the best of times or the worst of times, it's the only time we've got."

There is a story about an old Jewish rabbi who told his students that they should live any way they desired, so long as they repented of their sins the day before they died.

One of his students seemed puzzled by this statement. "But, Rabbi," he said, "we do not know what day we are going to die."

185

The rabbi nodded thoughtfully. "Then repent today," he said.

The point is that it is important to do whatever you want to do right now. Tomorrow may be too late.

Someone has said:

▲ If you want to know the value of one year, ask the student who has failed his final exam.

▲ If you want to know the value of one month, ask the mother who has given birth to a premature baby.

▲ To discover the value of one week, ask the editor of a weekly newspaper.

▲ To find out the value of one day, ask the daily wage laborer who has ten kids to feed.

▲ If you want to know the value of an hour, ask the lovers who are waiting to meet.

▲ If you want to know the value of a minute, ask the person who has just missed his plane.

▲ To discover the value of a second, ask the person who has survived an accident.

▲ To realize the value of a millisecond, ask the person who won a silver medal in the Olympics.

Yes, time is important, and we must strive not to get careless with it. Wasted seconds lead to wasted minutes, which lead to wasted hours, which eventually lead to wasted years and wasted lifetimes.

As the Jewish scribe Yelchaninov wrote: "Our continual mistake is that we do not concentrate upon the present day, the actual hour of our life. We live in the past or in the future. We are continually expecting the coming of some special hour, when our life shall unfold itself in its significance. We do not observe that life is flowing like water through our fingers, sifting like precious grain from a loosely-fastened bag."

Author Christopher Morley gives us plenty of food for thought when he says: "If we suddenly discovered that we had only five minutes left to say all we wanted to say, every telephone booth would be occupied by people trying to call other people to tell them that they loved them."

Many times when I'm speaking, I quote author Stephen Levine who said, "If you were going to die soon and had only one phone call you could make, who would you call and what would you say? And why are you waiting?"

Dr. Warren Wiersbe puts the exclamation point on it when he says, "In twenty years, what will you wish you had done today? Do it now!"

3. *Use today to begin to build your tomorrow.*

Having spent the better part of my adult life around professional athletes, I can say from experience that I believe there is no harder working group of people. I think especially of the 1999–2000 Orlando Magic, the hardest working group of men it's ever been my pleasure to be associated with. In sports, more than any other profession, you have to stay razor sharp at all times, because there is always a younger man (or woman) just itching to take your job.

The belief that professional athletes as a whole are spoiled, pampered, and lazy simply is not true. Of course, there are some players who fit that description, but most of them don't stay around very long. Professional sports demand constant attention, constant improvement, constant hard work.

I think of Michael Jordan and Larry Bird who, even when they were standing at the top of their profession, spent hundreds of hours in the off-season working to improve their skills. I think of Mark McGwire, hitting seventy home runs in a season yet still showing up early for batting practice because he was determined to do even better tomorrow than he was doing today.

These men understood that, as author William G. Carr wrote, "The shape of things to come is determined, not only by the past, but also, by every action or failure to act, in the present."

The Bible chooses the ant as an example of those who work hard today so their tomorrows will be good ones. Referring to the common insect, the Book of Proverbs advises the lazy man to "consider its ways and be wise! It has no commander, no overseer or ruler, yet it stores its provisions in summer and gathers its food at harvest" (Prov. 6:6–8).

187

Zig Ziglar may have been thinking of this verse when he wrote, "If you do the things you need to do when you need to do them, then, someday you can do the things you want to do, when you want to do them."

Harriet Marineu tells us that it is important to "live your best and act your best and think your best today, for today is the sure preparation for tomorrow and all the other tomorrows that follow."

And I especially like the advice given by poet Elizabeth Barrett Browning, who urges us to "light tomorrow with today."

So don't get distracted by tomorrow but remember that it's coming, and do what you can right now to make certain it's good when it gets here. Pleasant memories must be arranged for in advance.

Three Important Things to Remember about Tomorrow

1. *Tomorrow depends on the choices you make today.* You can't tell what's going to happen to you tomorrow. Your future is in God's hands, and no amount of preparation can guarantee it's going to consist of one triumphant moment on top of another. Sometimes, in this crazy, mixed-up world of ours, bad things happen to good people. Cancer strikes a woman who has always taken care of her body. Faulty wiring burns a house to the ground. A drunk driver crosses the center line and causes a head-on collision.

At the same time, good things sometimes happen to bad people. A greedy, abusive man may win several million dollars in the lottery. A woman who has never had an unselfish thought in her life may be blessed with a beautiful singing voice that makes her rich and famous.

And so it goes.

But even though such things happen, they are the exception to the rule. For the most part, the shape of the future is determined by the choices you make today. As someone who is very close to me (her name is Ruth) has said, "Winners make decisions that create their future. Losers make decisions that create their present. In other words, winners think about where they are going, and losers think about what they are going through."

Ralph Waldo Emerson was right when he said, "The future belongs to those who prepare for it." Or, as Jackie Joyner-Kersee said, "It is better to look ahead and prepare than to look back and regret."

I've read that the Iroquois Indians never made a major decision without thinking about how it would affect the tribe for the next seven generations. Decisions weren't based on, "Will this be good for us today?" but rather on, "Will this be good for our great grandchildren's great grandchildren?" Wouldn't it be great if we all thought this way? First, because it would prevent us from making decisions that would harm the future. Second, because it would motivate us to make decisions that, even though they may not pay off immediately, would have the potential to produce beneficial results for generations to come.

Don't you wish the people who are destroying our rain forests would stop to think about how their work will affect future generations? Such forward think- ing would have prevented many of the serious problems we face today: Water poisoned by toxic wastes, land ravaged by strip mining, and forests disappearing at an alarming rate.

Refusing to think about the future is like climbing a mountain without giving the slightest thought to how you're going to get back down. It's like destroying footholds and toeholds and obliterating landmarks so you can't use them again. It's more than foolish—it's dangerous!

▲

The future is something which everyone reaches at the rate of 60 minutes an hour, whatever he does, whoever he is.

C. S. LEWIS

▼

Walt Disney said that people who really want to accomplish something worthwhile must learn to think beyond their lifetimes. "Put together a 50-year master plan," he said. "Thinking 50 years ahead forces you to engage in a quality of thinking that will also improve your present thinking."

I've heard that the average American business bases its operations on a five-year plan, whereas it is not unusual for a successful com- pany in Japan to have a one-hundred-year plan. Will a one-hundred- year plan work? Consider this: Dr. Edward Banfield of Harvard Uni- versity spent several years studying the reasons why some families improve their economic standing from one generation to the next, while others do not. He came to the conclusion that the successful families maintained a long-term view of the future, while those who were unsuccessful did not. In other words, those who became successful made financial and other decisions based on how those choices would affect them several years from now. Members of the other group were generally more concerned with having fun in the short term than enjoying financial security over the long term. As a result, they made short-term choices that led to long-term hardships.

As you can see, long-term planning is important.

2. *The future is a journey, not a destination!* Someone asks, "When will it be time for me to stop and rest and be content with what I've done?" The answer is "Never."

Once you've reached the top of the mountain, it's good to stop, rest for awhile, and enjoy the view. Be happy with what you've done. And then start planning your next climb. There will always be one more mountain to climb, one more victory to win, one more goal to achieve.

Julius Erving, known during his days of stardom in the NBA as Doctor J., said that when some people reach the top of a mountain they think, "'I've done it, so now I need to just chill and live off my laurels.'" Then he added, "I can't sit back and spend the rest of my life having people tell me how good I used to be. The farther away I'm removed from it, the farther away it seems to me and the more important it is to be doing something that makes a difference now."

Remember that every achieved goal is only a temporary rest stop on the way to even greater achievements. Imagine a painter, lost in the passion of bringing his vision to the canvas. Which do you think would bring him the greatest joy—painting the picture, or seeing the finished product hanging on a wall in a gallery? Certainly, there is more joy in the act of creating.

When I say that the future is a journey, I also mean that we are moving into it, whether we want to or not. We cannot stay where we are—today—because tomorrow is constantly overtaking us! Climber John Amatt says, "It is impossible to stay where we are! If we become complacent and stagnate, or start to drift, we will be left behind by more aggressive people."

190

The choice is ours. We can move bravely into the future or we can let life sweep us along against our will. But one way or the other, we *will* be taking the journey.

3. *Keep your fork, the best is yet to come!*

Driving down a highway in South Carolina, I saw this sign in front of a small church: "Do not be afraid of tomorrow; God is already there."

Pastor Tony Evans once wrote, "Tomorrow is as real to God as today or yesterday because God is an eternal being. In fact time designations have no meaning to Him. He is forever in the present tense, the now." That's good to know, isn't it? None of us can see the future, but we can know for sure that whenever we get there, God will have been there ahead of us. And as long as he's there, what do we have to fear?

I heard a story about a dying woman who called her pastor to come to her house so they could discuss her burial wishes. The preacher was surprised when she told him she wanted to be buried with a fork in her hand. When he asked why, she explained, "Whenever there was a potluck supper at the church, my favorite part was when they said, 'keep your fork.' That always meant something great was coming for dessert. When people come to my funeral, I want them to remember that something better is coming for all of us who belong to God. They'll need to keep their forks."

So keep your fork. If you are a child of God, something better is on its way. Something much, much better!

Before we take our next step on our journey up the mountain, I want to share these words from Walter Fauntroy, former member of the House of Representatives from the District of Columbia. In a speech delivered to the graduating class at Howard University, he said, "The past is yours. Learn from it. The present is yours. Fulfill it. The future is yours. Preserve it. Knowledge is yours. Use it. Cancer is yours. Cure it. Racism is yours. End it. Do not be blinded by prejudice, disheartened by the times or discouraged by the system. Do not let anything paralyze your mind, tie your hands or defeat your spirit. Take the world, not to dominate it, but to deliver it; not to exploit it, but to enrich it. Take the dream and inherit the earth."

191

LIFE LESSON NUMBER TWO: HAVE FUN ALONG THE WAY

My dad instilled in us how essential it is to enjoy the process of life, regarding every moment and every act as having some importance. He taught us that's how people achieve greatness in whatever they do.

JILL TRANSKI, DAUGHTER OF CARTOONIST CHARLES SCHULZ

ARE YOU HAVING FUN YET?

I wasn't having much fun on the mountain. Let's be honest. I was miserable. I was lying on my bunk at Camp Muir, wishing I had a nice, warm electric blanket—and a place to plug it in—and thinking about what a long, hard, bitterly cold day it had been. I was ready to go home, and we were still 4,000 feet from the summit of Mount Rainier. And even after we got there, we'd still have to make it all the way back to camp.

"This is supposed to be my vacation," I thought, "and I'm not having any fun! I'm struggling! I'm cold! I'm miserable! I've got to do something about this!"

Well, the truth was there wasn't much I could do. I didn't have an electric blanket. I didn't know anyone with a helicopter who could zoom on up to Camp Muir and rescue me. It wasn't possible to pick up the phone, call, and have a hot pizza delivered. All I had were a few Power Bars. And they were frozen.

But then it hit me. There was one thing I could do! I could change my attitude! So that's what I did. I decided that I would focus on making this an adventure, on having the type of fun I thought I was going to have when I had first signed on to this mountain-climbing expedition.

It's amazing what a difference a change in attitude can make. We went out of that hut and began to climb through the night, and the mountain seemed far less hostile and much more awesome. I started enjoying the day. I was having fun.

I'm not saying that all of my troubles went away the instant I decided to change my thinking. I'd be lying if I said that was the case. It was still terribly cold on that mountain, but now, somehow, that seemed to add to my sense of adventure. The climb was still difficult, but now I welcomed the challenge. I was enjoying every new experience that came my way.

Are you having fun in life? If not, there are two things you can do:

1. You can do what I did, and change your attitude.
2. You can change what you're doing.

Regarding the first option, Dr. Albert Schweitzer said, "Success is not the key to happiness. Happiness is the key to success. If you love what you are doing, you will be successful."

As for the second option, William Stavropoulos, CEO of Dow Chemical, said, "If you really don't have enthusiasm for something, make a change, whether it's in a job, a company, or even a career."

Wouldn't it be great to be able to look back over your life someday and say, as Thomas Edison did, "I never worked a day in my life. It was all fun!"

The bottom line? Climbing a mountain is supposed to be fun and enjoyable, so don't take it so seriously. Loosen the bow strings and have some fun every day. As someone has said, "When you're walking on thin ice, you might as well dance!"

San Francisco sports writer Scott Ostler proposes that we set aside a national holiday to honor the memory of two of the twentieth century's greatest high-livers—Babe Ruth and Elvis Presley—both of whom died on August 16. Ostler says that the difference between this day and every other national holiday would be that, instead of taking the day off, everyone would "take the day on. Swing from the heels, sing from the heart, live larger, dream bigger, eat more, sleep less, break new ground, break old rules, break a record, cut a record, cut a swath." You know what? I think Scott Ostler is really on to something here.

The late columnist Erma Bombeck was once asked what she would do differently if she had her life to live over again. She said, "There would be more I love you's, more I'm sorry's, more I'm listening's; but mostly, given another shot at life, I would seize every minute of it—look at it and really see it—try it on—live it—exhaust it—and never give that minute back until there was nothing left of it."

I think Erma Bombeck was a wise woman. We should all learn to have fun right now, in this present minute, to take whatever joy life has to offer. "Relish the moment" would be a very good motto to live by. Far too many people go through life believing that they're going to have great pleasure "someday," but they don't get any fun or enjoyment out of life right now.

As you climb your mountain, I urge you to do your best to get the most fun you can out of every step you take. Always remember that the journey toward success should be as much fun as actually achieving success. The late climber Alex Lowe said, "The best climber in the world is the one who's having the most fun."

Lene Gammelgaard, who has reached the summit of Mount Everest several times, says she has a painting of a clown on her door to remind her to enjoy what she is doing. She adds that "even though climbing Mount Everest is serious business, it's only considered news for a short while. In a hundred years it's all forgotten . . . so, it's all about enjoying the journey of life. . . ."

Another experienced Everest climber, the late George Leigh Mallory, agreed with that assessment. When asked what benefit is to be obtained from climbing a mountain like Everest, Mallory said, "What we get from this adventure is just sheer joy, and joy is, after all, the end of life."

Some people spend their lives wishing great things would happen to them—that they would win the lottery, get signed to a major league contract, write a best-seller, or come up with an invention that makes them rich and famous. They are so busy thinking about this sort of thing that they miss the fun that comes out of everyday life—the beauty of a sunset, the music in the laughter of a child, a cup of hot cider on a winter's day, a moonlit night. These are the small pleasures that are there for all of us to take and enjoy, and it is a tragedy to miss them.

▲

Laughter is the joyous universal evergreen of life.

ABRAHAM LINCOLN

▼

Robert Hastings writes that many of us tend to think we will be happy someday— "When I am eighteen," "When I buy a Porsche," "When I put the last kid through college," "When I have paid off the mortgage," and so on. Then he adds, "Sooner or later, we must realize there is no station; no one place to arrive at, once and for all. The true joy of life outdistances us. So, stop packing the aisle and counting the miles. Instead, climb more mountains, eat more ice cream, go barefoot more often, swim more rivers, watch more sunsets, laugh more, cry less. Life must be lived as we go along."

Here are four important things you need to remember about having fun:

1. Our forebears had a sense of humor.
2. Having fun is good for your health.
3. Having fun increases, rather than decreases, efficiency.
4. It's fun to be you—so relax and be yourself!

Once again, let's take a closer look:

1. Our Forebears Had a Sense of Humor

Where do we get the idea that the great men and women of history were humorless, driven types who never had a moment of enjoyment? It's simply not true! Theodore Roosevelt told his sons that the best advice he could give them was "Have all the fun you can." Doesn't sound very much like an old stick-in-the-mud to me.

In September of 1862 Abraham Lincoln called a special session of his advisors, telling them he had an important matter he wanted to discuss with them. When the men arrived, they were surprised to find the president chuckling over an article by Artemus Ward, one of the best-known humorists of his day. The article was titled "A High-Handed Outrage at Utica," and Lincoln thought it was so funny that he read it aloud to the assembled group.

When he had finished, Lincoln threw back his head and roared with laughter. But he seemed to be the only one in the room who found the article even mildly amusing. The others seemed to be embarrassed and even ashamed that the President could be having so much fun during a time when the country was torn by civil war.

Lincoln shook his head. "Why don't you laugh?" he asked. "With the fearful strain that is upon me night and day, if I did not laugh, I should die, and you need this medicine as much as I do."

Then he turned his attention to the "important matter" he wanted to discuss with them—the first draft of the Emancipation Proclamation.

Tom Monaghan, founder of Domino's Pizza, tried for years to set up a meeting with his hero, Ray Kroc, founder of McDonald's. Once a month for several years, Monaghan called Kroc's office trying to set up an appointment, but Kroc was never available. Then, when Monaghan heard that his seventy-eight-year-old hero was in failing health, he flew to San Diego, where Kroc lived, determined that he would not leave until a meeting had been arranged.

The two men hit it off immediately, and the fifteen minutes Kroc had set aside for the meeting continued for two and a half hours. Near the end of their conversation, Kroc leaned forward in his chair and said, "I'm going to give you some advice. You have it made now. You can do anything you want; make all the money you can possibly spend. So what I think you should do now is slow down. Take it easy. Open a few stores every year, but be careful. Play it safe."

Monaghan was disappointed. "But that wouldn't be any fun!" he said.

Kroc broke into a huge grin. "That's just what I hoped you'd say," he said.

Just a couple of fellows who know how to have a good time!

America has given much laughter to the rest of the world. We are the home of Laurel and Hardy, W. C. Fields, the Marx Brothers, the Three Stooges, Abbott and Costello, Martin and Lewis, Burns and Allen, Lucille Ball, Robin Williams, Jay Leno . . . and the list could go on and on. This country has made many marvelous contributions to people everywhere—and I believe the gift of laughter is right up there with the best of them.

> ▲
>
> The simple truth is that happy people generally don't get sick.
>
> DR. BERNIE SIEGEL
>
> ▼

That's why I like very much what Garrison Keillor, of *The Prairie Home Companion* radio show, had to say to today's graduates: "I am less worried about our vision and our industry than I am about our lack of humor. The greatness of America is that it produces exuberant geniuses such as Louis Armstrong and Fred Astaire and John Updike and Leonard Bernstein. We are meant to be a jazzy people who talk big talk and jump up on the table and dance. We aren't supposed to be dopey and glum and brood over old injuries. Laughter is what proves our humanity, and the ability to give a terrific party is a sign of true class."

2. Having Fun Is Good for Your Health

The *Reader's Digest* has a department called "Laughter Is the Best Medicine." That's a paraphrase from the seventeenth chapter of Proverbs, which tells us that a "cheerful heart" is good medicine (v. 22). It's true that laughter does a body good. It stirs up the blood, expands the chest, electrifies the nerves, and clears away the cobwebs from the brain.

So if you are climbing a mountain, you'd better see to it that you have fun and laugh a lot. After all, you're going to need all the strength you can get!

When editor and writer Norman Cousins was diagnosed with an incurable disease, he arranged to have videotapes of the old *Candid Camera* show played for him. The videos made Cousins howl with laughter, and that, in turn, pumped strength into his body. In his book *Anatomy of an Illness*, Cousins tells how, the more he turned to laughter as a healer, his pain decreased, he slept better, and he generally felt better, physically and emotionally.

Dr. William Fry Jr., explains: "Laughter is a form of physical exercise. It causes huffing and puffing, accelerates the heart rate, raises blood pressure, speeds up breathing, increases oxygen consumption, exercises the muscles of the face and stomach, and relaxes muscles not involved in laughing. It stimulates the liver, stomach, pancreas, spleen and gall bladder. In short, the entire body gets an invigorating lift." He said that laughing heartily one hundred times a day has the same positive effect on the body as ten minutes on a rowing machine.

According to humorist Herm Albright, during a good belly laugh, a person's heart rate can top 120 beats per minute. "So laugh it up," he says. "It's good for you."

Wow! Anybody know a good joke?

When Charity Lawson reached her ninety-fifth birthday, the Sweetwater, Texas, woman was asked the secret to her longevity. She replied, "I've always liked to have a good time. You've got to have fun."

That's just about what I would have expected her to say. I've never heard of an elderly person looking back on his or her life and saying, "You know, I think I had too much fun. If I had it all to do over again, I think I'd laugh a little less and try to take things more seriously. I'd cut out some of the silly stuff and spend more time in the office."

You know why that doesn't happen? Because old age brings wisdom. And wisdom shows you how important it is to have as much fun as you can every day.

Comedian Bob Hope, closing in on his one hundredth birthday, says, "Everyone tells you that diet and exercise are the secret to long life, but laughter is. Laughter is therapy . . . an instant vacation." Hope also said that when he looks back on his life, it's not his many moments in the spotlight that bring him the most joy. Instead, he remembers, "quiet moments with my family, unwinding on the golf course, convivial times with old friends. In short, having fun."

Late-night television host Conan O'Brien says, "Laughter is an anesthetic. I could get shot five times and, if people think it's funny, I won't even feel it." Perhaps he's exaggerating. But then again, perhaps not!

Author Eugene Griessman says that whenever something bad happens to you, the best way to bounce back from the brink of disaster is to learn to laugh about it. He writes: "The ability to see something funny in your misfortunes is an important coping skill. Begin by smiling. That's right. Physically put a smile on your face. You will discover that it's almost impossible to feel depressed when you are engaged in smiling."

He goes on, "The next step is stimulating laughter—at least a chuckle. If you can do something to make you laugh, you have taken a giant step toward defeating negative, defeatist attitudes. Laughter increases blood circulation, feeds oxygen to the brain, pumps out hormones that aid alertness, and releases pain-killing endorphins."

In Tallahassee, Florida, recently, I saw this sign outside a business: "You don't quit playing because you grow old. You grow old because you quit playing." Amen!

As writer Anne Wilson Schaef says, "I realize that humor isn't for everyone. It's only for people who want to have fun, enjoy life, and feel alive."

3. Having Fun Increases, Rather Than Decreases, Efficiency

Good old Dagwood Bumstead, always hanging around the watercooler, wasting the company's time and money. He's enough to drive a boss to distraction! No wonder Mr. Dithers has to give him a swift kick in the seat of the pants every now and then to get him to go back to work!

Well, guess what, Mr. Dithers. The latest research tells us that it's actually good for the company if Dagwood spends some time around the watercooler, having fun with his buddies. That's right! People who take a little time to "goof off" at work every once in awhile, are actually more productive than those "nose-to-the-grindstone" types! Having some fun invigorates them. It gets the blood pumping so they have more energy when they get back to the task at hand. Because they enjoy being at work more, they are also likely to do a better job at whatever they do.

Is there such a thing as having too much fun? Of course. I'm not suggesting for a moment that it's okay to fritter the day away without doing anything constructive. But fun with reasonable limits is not only acceptable, it's beneficial, and almost indispensable. I really love this quote from historian Arnold Toynbee: "The supreme accomplishment is to blur the line between work and play."

It's sad but true that most people feel guilty about having fun when they're supposed to be working. They may even think, *I can't be doing this job right. I'm having too much fun.* Somewhere along the way, we picked up the idea that work and fun can't have anything to do with each other, and that's nonsense.

Martha Ingram, CEO of Ingram Industries, recognizes the importance of fun in the workplace. She says, "I want people to love to come to work. I want them to have a good time." She adds, "I think a sense of fun can be good. People become more productive."

▲

Work should be fun! That outrageous assertion is the value that fuels the most productive people and companies in this country.

BEST-SELLING AUTHOR JOHN NAISMITH

▼

The night before U.S. softball star Dr. Dot Richardson left for the 2000 Olympics in Sydney, Australia, my wife and I were out for an evening of bowling with the kids at a spot near Orlando. Dr. Dot was there and came over to greet us and pour some of her enthusiasm into our lives. You talk about an athlete living life to the fullest and having fun while she's doing it!

201

The next day writer David Whitley had a feature story on Dot in the *Orlando Sentinel,* in which he quoted her: "Every minute that goes by is a minute that's lost if we don't enjoy it. Your life can be as exciting as you want it to be. I love my life. Yes, it's demanding. Yes, there's not a lot of sleep. But the fun I'm having outweighs those small little technicalities. Slow down and take a vacation? How fun would that be? I can't do a vacation. There's too much to do."

Dave Thomas, founder of Wendy's and star of dozens of humorous television commercials, has this to say: "You know what I think can be one of the best motivators of all in the workplace? Fun. I'm not talking about reckless horseplay, but good clean, harmless fun . . . like a family might do."

Thomas's point is a good one. When I talk about "fun," I do not mean having a good time at someone else's expense. Sexual harassment does not fall into the category of fun. Neither does mean-spiritedness of any kind.

Dr. Christian Hagaset III has come up with an excellent list of appropriate ways to use humor in the workplace. Among the things he says we should do:

▲ Use humor for positive, playful, uplifting, healing, and loving purposes.

▲ Take ourselves lightly, even while we take our work seriously.

▲ Avoid taking offense at another's attempt at humor, always giving them the benefit of the doubt and believing that they meant well.

▲ Refuse to use humor to camouflage hostility or prejudice.

▲ Laugh generously at another's attempt to use humor, understanding that laughter is a treasured gift.

▲ Respect the forbidden topics of coworkers, and make amends if offense is taken.

▲ In the midst of adversity, use humor to cope, to survive, to heal, to grow, and to pass on love and kindness.

Billy Graham said, "A keen sense of humor helps us to overlook the unbecoming, understand the unconventional, tolerate the unpleasant, overcome the unexpected and outlast the unbearable." Sounds like it will come in pretty handy at the office, don't you think?

Dave Longaberger, CEO of the company that bears his name has come to this conclusion: "Having a good time is the best motivator there is. When people feel good about a company, they produce more."

Tom Peters, who is widely recognized as one of the world's foremost experts on business, agrees. "Business ought to be fun." Executive John Sculley says, "People are going to be most productive when they are doing something they're really interested in. So having fun isn't an outrageous idea at all. It is a very sensible one."

Another business executive who has found that happy people are productive people is Herb Kelleher, the head of Southwest Airlines. (Hmmm . . . another company with funny commercials!) Among other things, Kelleher has appeared at corporate headquarters dressed as Elvis Presley, boarded a flight in an Easter Bunny costume, and painted one of his planes to look like Shamu, the killer whale of Sea World fame.

Kelleher explains how he hires new people for his airline: "What we are looking for first and foremost is a sense of humor." He explains further, "You shouldn't have to change your personality when you come to work. At Southwest, we have created an atmosphere where we hire good people, let them be themselves, and pay a great deal of attention to them and their personal lives. In other words, we create an environment where people can really enjoy what they are doing."

▲

Every rule in the book can be broken except one. Be who you are, and become all you were meant to be....

SYDNEY J. HARRIS

▼

Has it worked? Apparently so. Southwest has been America's most consistently profitable airline—with profits increasing on a yearly basis. And Kelleher was referred to as "America's best CEO" by *Fortune* magazine.

The next time someone tells you that work and fun don't mix, tell them to get in touch with Herb Kelleher. He knows different.

4. It's Fun to Be You—So Relax and Be Yourself (Everyone Else Is Taken)!

When my son Alan was thirteen years old, his teacher asked her students to write a statement on the subject, "If you could be anyone in the world, who would you like to be?"

Alan wrote: "Myself, because God made me this way, and I'm proud of who I am."

I was proud of his answer and glad that Alan didn't want to be some superstar athlete or rock star. Being happy with who you are is an important ingredient of personal success. And sadly, in today's world where fame, beauty, power, and financial success seem to be valued above all else, finding someone who is satisfied with "just being me," is becoming increasingly difficult. As Malcolm Forbes said, "Too many people over-value what they are not, and under-value what they are."

Writer-pastor Dr. Tony Evans says, "Wanting to be like somebody else is not your calling." He goes on to explain, "God only has one of you. If He wanted you to copy someone else, He would have made you that person's identical twin. God has customized His calling for your life so that, when you come to the end, you can say you have finished the work God gave you to do."

It would have been ridiculous for me, as I was climbing up Mount Rainier, to act as if I thought I was Sir Edmund Hillary, or some other great, skilled adventurer. I was me, Pat Williams, a novice climber, learning something new—about life, about my own endurance, about mountains. Only by admitting that I was new at mountain climbing—by being totally open to what others could show me and teach me—was I able to get the most from my experience.

Frank Robinson, who was elected to the National Baseball Hall of Fame on the first ballot, tasted success both as a major league player and manager. During spring training of his first year as manager of the San Francisco Giants, a reporter asked him whom he patterned himself after when he was first starting out as a player.

The reporter thought Robinson was joking when he replied, "I tried to be like Frank Robinson."

"C'mon," the reporter said. "Who was it, really?"

"Look," Robinson said, "the most important person any player should work to be as good as is himself. Your own excellence, success and greatest pride come from only one person—you." Robinson says it's fine to look up to and learn from someone else, but "your first responsibility is to be the best you can be. There's nobody else like you so why try to be like somebody else?

"You might be surprised to find out how much better you can be," he concluded.

Brooke Shields had the opposite experience: "I was guilty of comparing myself with others all the time. I'd look in magazines and look at other models and compare myself with them; same thing with actresses. I had to learn that we are different and just can't be someone else, or even try to be. I had to learn to appreciate myself."

As e.e. cummings said, "To be nobody but myself . . . in a world which is doing its best, night and day, to make you everybody else . . . means to fight the hardest battle which any human being can fight, and never stop fighting."

It is a constant surprise to me how many bright, intelligent, attractive, and witty people suffer from low self-esteem! In fact just yesterday I heard on the news that a new study has concluded that the more intelligent a person is, the more likely he or she is to have low self-esteem! I think that's amazing. It almost seems that people who ought to feel the best about themselves feel the worst. Do you think you don't have much to offer the world? That may just be a sign of how smart you are!

Please remember that you are unique, a special creation of God. There is nobody else like you. Nobody else can do what you can do. Nobody else can have the impact on this world that you can!

Just think of all the billions and billions of snowflakes that have fallen on this planet since the creation. And yet science tells us that no two of them have ever been alike. There are over five billion people alive right now, and no two share the same fingerprints.

Human beings are more unique, more "wonderfully made," and far more complex than snowflakes or fingerprints. Nobody can speak with your voice, smile with your smile, or touch the lives you are meant to touch. As someone has said, "If you are not there to shine your light, who knows how many travelers will lose their way as they try to pass by your empty place in the darkness?"

Holocaust survivor Elie Weisel says, "When we die and go to Heaven, our Maker is not going to say, 'Why didn't you discover the cure for such and such?' The only thing we're going to be asked at that precious moment is, 'Why didn't you become you?'"

As the great English writer Samuel Johnson put it, "No man is great by imitation." Or, as the late Judy Garland said, "Always be a first-rate version of yourself instead of a second-rate version of somebody else."

In their book *Soul Food*, Jack Kornfield and Christina Feldman tell a story about eight-year-old Molly, who went out to a fancy restaurant to have dinner with her family.

After the rest of the family had ordered, the waiter turned to Molly and asked, "And what do you want?"

"A hot dog and a soda," she said.

Her grandmother shook her head. "She'll have the roast chicken dinner, with carrots and mashed potatoes."

"And milk to drink," said her father.

The waiter turned back to Molly.

"And would you like ketchup or mustard on your hot dog?" he asked.

"Ketchup!" she shouted.

Then, as the waiter walked away, little Molly turned to her family, her eyes wide with delight and surprise. "You know what?" she said. "He thinks I'm real!"

You know what else? You are real too. You are important—to God, to other people, to yourself, and to the entire world, because you're a part of God's plan for the world. Remember that, and it will speed your trip up the mountain.

LIFE LESSON NUMBER ONE: CONCENTRATE ON CHARACTER

During my 87 years, I have witnessed a succession of technologi-
cal revolutions, but none of them has done away with the need for
character. . . .

BERNARD BARUCH

DALLAS GREEN IS AN IMPOSING FIGURE of a man. He stands 6'5"
and weighs 250 pounds—give or take a few. I can still hear him
shouting, when he was manager of the Philadelphia Phillies: "I
want character people on this team!" Of course, he wanted players on his team who could hit, catch, and throw the ball. He wanted
men who could run the bases and who had the desire to win. But
most of all, he wanted players who were willing to sacrifice their
individual glory for the good of the team, men who were willing
to give everything they had to become winners, men who believed

in fair play and sportsmanship, men who were winners on and off the field. He wanted men of character.

Before the Arizona Diamondbacks took the field for the first time in 1998, manager Buck Showalter said, "We drafted character players." No wonder the Diamondbacks captured the National League West pennant in 1999, in only their second year of existence.

Dallas Green and Buck Showalter both understood that character is a vitally important component of success—in sports or any other field of endeavor. Character counts in sports. It counts in business. It counts in law. It counts in the medical profession. It counts in *every* profession. It counts in a family. It counts in school. And it especially counts on a mountain.

Character can make all the difference in the world when the cold wind is blowing, the wet snow is coming down so fast you can't see ten feet in front of you, and the lack of oxygen in the air has you gasping for breath!

Make no mistake, the mountain will reveal your character—strengths and flaws alike. When you're out there on the snow and ice, battling the wind and cold, taking orders from demanding guides, counting on (and being counted on by) your teammates, you learn and reveal a lot about yourself.

I once heard Jim Henry, our pastor at First Baptist Church, Orlando, remark that "character is not something you have; it is something you are that shows itself in what you do."

Mountain climber Sue Cobb felt she never could reach the summit of Mount Everest without being a person of character. She wrote in her book *The Edge of Everest:* "Everest is a symbol of excellence, of the barely attainable. It is the mightiest challenge: a brutal struggle with rock, ice, altitude and self. The satisfaction comes from enduring the struggle, from doing more than you thought you could do, from rising—however briefly—above your everyday world, and from coming, momentarily, closer to the stars."

Some people will tell you that a person's character is being formed when he or she is out there on the mountain, but I don't believe that's necessarily true. Mountains don't create character. They simply reveal, and strengthen, the character that's already there.

Think about the people you know who have gone through difficult times. How did they react? Some people probably became

208

more patient, more understanding toward others, more certain of God's goodness. The character traits that were already present in their lives were brought out and magnified. Others probably became more angry, bitter, impatient, and cynical toward God. Again, the difficulty in their lives didn't make them that way—it just amplified the traits that were already there.

And yet it's important to understand that character is more than just an innate personality trait, something you can't help. Strength of character can be developed, like physical strength that comes from regular exercise. As author James A. Froude said, "You cannot dream yourself into character; you must hammer and forge one for yourself."

I was recently at a swimming meet with my children and I liked the slogan I saw printed on the back of the T-shirt one of the coaches was wearing. I liked it so much, in fact, that I stopped right there and wrote it down: "Results bring status—the journey builds character."

That's pretty much what life's journey is all about—building character and becoming all we can be, fulfilling the potential that God has placed inside us.

In this chapter, we're going to talk about the nine qualities that people with character possess. They are:

1. Faith
2. Honesty and integrity
3. A strong work ethic
4. Maturity
5. Responsibility
6. Perseverance
7. Humility
8. Influence
9. Courage

209

Somebody asks, "Do I have to have all of these traits to be a person of character?" Absolutely! This is not a menu from a Chinese restaurant where you can pick one from column A, another from column B, and so on. Suppose you have eight of these traits but you're lacking one of them—humility, perhaps, or courage, or faith, which I believe to be the most important trait of all. If you are lacking even a single one of these traits, your life is not what it could and should be.

For example, can you get to the top of the mountain without faith? Of course, but the experience won't be everything it could be. You won't stand up on the mountain with your nostrils flaring and your hair flying in the breeze, feeling exhilarated in body, mind, and spirit. Instead, you're likely to be standing at the top of the mountain feeling disappointed and wondering, "Why do I feel so empty?"

I'll say it again. In order for your life to be everything it can and should be, you must have all of the nine character traits listed above.

Let's take a closer look.

1. Faith

As I've already said, I believe that faith in Jesus Christ is the most important character trait a person can have. It helps in so many areas of life.

During the 1950s and '60s, Bobby Richardson was an outstanding second baseman for the world champion New York Yankees. He was also a committed Christian who talked openly about his faith. A reporter once asked him if being a Christian made him a better baseball player. Richardson thought for a moment and then said something like this: "Well, being a Christian makes me a better teammate. It makes me a better husband. And it makes me a better father. And I would think that all of that *has* to make me a better baseball player!"

I've had some very difficult experiences in my life, as most of us have, and I don't know how I would have made it thus far without my faith in Jesus Christ to sustain and comfort me. Faith gives you an eternal perspective. It reminds you that no matter what you are passing through, it is only temporary. Faith holds on to God's promises that the day is coming when "He will wipe every tear from their eyes. There will be no more death or mourning or crying or pain, for the old order of things has passed away" (Rev. 21:4).

I'm not sure why, but there's no place in the world I felt quite as close to God as I did when I was on that mountain. I know I'm not alone in this. In fact the spiritual exhilaration that comes from being on a mountain has become part of our everyday language. We speak of joyous moments in our lives as "mountaintop experiences."

The first reason why climbing a mountain can be a faith-building experience is because mountains are such a spectacular part of God's creation. When I'm on a mountain, all I have to do is look around me and I'm instantly reminded of God's power, majesty, and creativity.

The second reason for the "spiritual high" associated with mountains may be the fact that—as reading through almost any book of the Bible will reveal—mountains have always had a special significance to God. Perhaps he still comes to meet us in a special way when we're on a pilgrimage to the summit of his creation. There are over five hundred references to mountains in the Bible, and many of those mountains have played an important role in God's dealings with mankind. For example:

> ▲
>
> It's been my faith, more than anything else, that has enabled me to keep my perspective and not feel devastated or bitter when things have gone wrong. It's that faith that gives me hope for whatever the future holds for me.
>
> TOM LANDRY
>
> ▼

Mount Ararat is where the ark landed after the great flood.

Mount Sinai is where God met with Moses and gave him the Ten Commandments.

Mount Nebo afforded Moses his only view of the Promised Land.

Mount Zion, just outside Jerusalem, is often referred to in the Scriptures as "God's holy mountain."

211

It was on the *Mount of Olives* that Jesus delivered one of his best-known sermons.

And, finally, it was on *Mount Calvary*, at a place known as Golgotha, that Jesus was crucified, thus bridging the gap that sin had put between God and man.

Yes, the mountains in our lives can teach us much about God if we will let them. I would go so far as to say that a mountain is one of the great natural evidences of God's existence. But faith is not something that can be arrived at solely on the basis of evidence. Faith requires making a decision to believe that God exists. Happily, millions of people have discovered that, once that decision is made, God proves it to be the right one.

After a swim meet not too long ago, my kids decided they wanted pancakes for brunch. So we all piled into my new car and headed down the highway, looking for an International House of Pancakes. After we drove along for awhile and didn't see one, Ruth said, "Why don't you try that new gadget of yours?"

Good idea.

She was talking about the "Onstar System" that came with the car. With the simple push of a button, the Onstar System can connect you to a "real person" at a central location who can give you directions, make dinner reservations, do all sorts of wonderful things.

So I pressed the button.

"Hello, Mr. Williams," said a friendly voice. "My name is Tia. How may I help you?"

About this time, the kids' mouths were gaping open in wonder.

"Well, Tia," I said, "We're looking for an International House of Pancakes."

It took her only a few seconds to respond. "I see you're traveling east on Route 436 in Altamonte Springs—and if you keep going another three miles, you'll see the restaurant."

"Can you tell me what side of the highway it's on?"

"No, sir. I'm not able to determine that."

Sure enough, three miles more and there it was!

212

At that moment, I would have been delighted to do a commercial for the Onstar System. But it got me to thinking that we all have an "Onstar connection" to the heavenly Father.

He knows where we are and where we're going. He sees the big picture and knows how we can get to where we want and need to be.

He's ready and willing to give guidance, and all we have to do is believe that he's there! He's always ready to listen. You don't even have to push a button. If you have not made the decision to "have faith in God," why not make it right now?

Chuck Swindoll says, "There is nothing more important about us than what we think about God. It shapes our moral and ethical standards; it affects our responses to pain and hardship; it motivates our response towards fame, power and pleasure; it gives us strength when we are tempted; it keeps us faithful and courageous. . . ." He goes on to say that faith is "the foundation upon which everything rests," and he is correct.

As Chuck Colson, president and founder of Prison Fellowship Ministries, says, "Success is . . . believing, following and serving God, and being at peace with Him."

Having faith in God doesn't mean that everything is going to go your way. It simply means that you will have his peace and joy even on those days when you wonder why you ever got out of bed! Even when the mountain wins, leaving you shaking your fist and waiting for

▲

I hope I shall possess firmness and virtue enough to maintain what I consider the most enviable of all titles, the character of an honest man.

GEORGE WASHINGTON

▼

another day to try again, faith in God can be a source of joy, strength, and peace.

I love what A. C. Green of the Los Angeles Lakers says about faith in Christ: "The more we become like Christ, the more goals we'll reach. He wants us to win, so He leads us into championship living. We win, inwardly, when we measure up, to the best of our ability, to the standard He sets for us. It may take years for others to see our championship qualities and acknowledge them, but the inner peace, character, strength, obedience and other championship qualities God places within us will show up eventually."

2. Honesty and Integrity

General Colin Powell has a very special memento in his home. It's a framed photograph of himself with President Ronald Reagan. Mr. Reagan inscribed it: "Colin, when you tell me something, I know it is so." What a tribute to Colin Powell's honesty and integrity.

Thomas Jefferson said that whenever he made decisions, even those made in private behind closed doors, he imagined that everyone he respected was watching him. In that way, he could be certain that he was doing the honest thing.

I think that was a very good idea. Why? Because human nature being what it is, it's not always easy to be honest. It often seems easier, or more beneficial, to lie. Every day most of us are presented with dozens of opportunities to tell the hard truth or take the easy way out with a lie. As we make the decision to tell the truth time after time after time, integrity is burned into our character. Honesty becomes a habit. And, as author Ivor Griffith said, "Character is a victory, not a gift."

Here are three ways you can build integrity into your character:

▲ Stand up for what you believe in, even when others are pressuring you to do otherwise.
▲ Be sure to give other people credit that rightfully belongs to them.

214

▲ Don't try to fool others into thinking you're something you're not. Be yourself.

Some of us have taught our children that telling the truth always brings rewards. Unfortunately that's not true insofar as the world views rewards. We all know liars who seem to get away with it, cheaters who prosper, people who've padded their resumes with degrees, awards, and experience they never really obtained. Often it's the dishonest man who seems to prosper, while the man of integrity is held back or even ostracized because of his truthfulness.

I've read that cheating seems to be nearing epidemic proportions among today's high school and college students. It's no wonder when lying and cheating seem to be easy ways to get to the top.

Business guru Tom Peters spoke at a seminar in Orlando that I attended. I will always remember his comment that "there are no minor lapses of integrity." There are at least three reasons integrity is important as we climb life's mountains:

▲

Genius is one percent inspiration and ninety-nine percent perspiration.

THOMAS EDISON

▼

- ▲ God sees our honesty and is pleased by it.
- ▲ Integrity builds strength of character that produces benefits in every area of life.
- ▲ If we lie about our abilities, if we say we're ready to climb the mountain when we're really not, we will ultimately fail, big. And when we're trying to climb a mountain, failure can be fatal!

3. A Strong Work Ethic

After hearing Ludwig Van Beethoven play the piano, a woman gushed to him, "It was magic! You're a genius!"

The great composer smiled and responded, "If you practiced playing the piano eight hours a day for forty years, you'd be a genius too."

215

Smart-alecky? Perhaps. But also very true. Michelangelo said something very similar: "If people knew how hard I worked to get my mastery, it wouldn't seem so wonderful after all."

Jerry Krause of the Chicago Bulls has this plaque in his office: "Effort: The man on top of the mountain didn't fall there."

Ted Williams, arguably the best hitter in modern baseball history, said he had hit more baseballs in practice than anyone, except perhaps Ty Cobb. "I don't say it to brag," he said. "I just state it as a fact. From the time I was eleven years old, I've taken every possible opportunity to swing at a ball. I've swung and I've swung and I've swung." It's no surprise that no player since Ted Williams in 1941 has hit more than .400 over a full season.

Years ago I was in Seattle to speak at a convention and I stayed at the same hotel as the Utah Jazz, who were there to play the Sonics. In the hotel weight room, I was surprised to run into Jazz superstar Karl Malone, who lifted weights for a full hour.

When I asked him why he worked so hard, he said, "It's the best way to stay ready. As I get older, I have to work harder." He smiled and added, "Besides, I've got to go against Shawn Kemp tomorrow night."

Karl Malone knows that there are no stairs to the top of a mountain, no escalator or elevator to get you to the summit. The only way to get there is through hard work!

> ▲
>
> Maturity is . . . the ability to sweat out a project or a situation, in spite of heavy opposition and discouraging setbacks, and stick with it until finished.
>
> ANN LANDERS
>
> ▼

Recently I had lunch with a prominent Orlando business leader and at the end of the session he told me a story about his ten-year-old son, Alan. He was putting his son to bed when Alan said, "Dad, when you die, will I get half your money?"

The man was shocked and responded, "Why would you ask me that question, son?"

Alan said, "Well, Dad, you are getting kind of old and I just wanted to know."

The father replied, "Son, rather than my giving you half the money, wouldn't you rather go out there by yourself and work hard to earn your own way? Wouldn't that be more fulfilling than my just giving you the money?"

Alan thought for a while and then said, "Dad, I'd rather you just give it to me."

There's an old story about a kingdom that was passing through a time of deep financial poverty. The king summoned his wisest economists and asked them to prepare some materials on the subject to help him understand why his kingdom was in trouble.

A year later, they returned with eighty-seven volumes. The angry monarch had half the economists executed and ordered the others to try again. Several months later, they came back and told him they had reduced all their work to four volumes.

Again, the king ordered half of them executed and told the survivors to keep trying. This went on until there was only one advisor left alive.

He prostrated himself before the king and said, "Sir, in only nine words I will reveal to you all the wisdom that I have distilled through all these years from all the writings of the economists who once practiced their science in your kingdom."

The king waited impatiently to hear the man's words of wisdom. "Well?" he demanded.

The advisor bowed low: "Your majesty . . . here is my text: 'There ain't no such thing as a free lunch.'"

Succinct, right to the point, and absolutely right.

4. Maturity

Another important aspect of a person's character is maturity. And when I say "maturity" I do not necessarily mean "age." I have known some people in their early twenties who exhibited tremendous maturity. I have also known people in their fifties and sixties who were reckless, immature, and displayed an amazing lack of good judgment. Maturity has more to do with what you've learned from the experiences you've had in life than it does with how many experiences you've had. Some people seem to go through experience piled on top of experience and never learn a thing. The world of sports is strewn with the bodies of those who ruined their careers, and their lives, because they kept making the same mistakes over and over again. They didn't learn. They didn't grow. They didn't become mature.

On a mountain, in the middle of a snowstorm, it takes maturity to realize that you have to keep on moving slowly and deliberately toward your goal—rest-stepping and pressure-breathing—when your tendency would be to run for shelter. Run, and you can quickly become disoriented and exhausted. This is only one of many such situations where a lack of maturity can bring failure and death.

▲

You cannot escape the responsibility of tomorrow by evading it today.

ABRAHAM LINCOLN

▼

Motivational speaker Jim Cathcart says that maturity "is being able to get yourself to do what needs to be done, when it needs to be done, whether you feel like it or not, and still do it well."

I've also heard it said that true maturity comes only when you finally realize that no one is coming to your rescue, so you're going to have to take care of yourself.

Maturity is being able to pass up instant gratification for the sake of long-term rewards. Maturity is the ability to see the big picture and not lose patience when the small details of life don't go your way. Maturity is the ability to stick with a job, a marriage, or a friendship even when you're passing through difficult times. And finally, maturity is the capacity to face unpleasantness, frustration, discomfort, and defeat without complaint or collapse. Mature people know they can't have everything their way all the time, but that's okay, because they care as much about others as they do about themselves. Author John MacNaughton put it this way: "Maturity begins to grow when you can sense your concern for others outweighing your concern for yourself." Mature people make it to the top of the mountain *together!*

5. Responsibility

Winston Churchill said that responsibility is the price of greatness.

218

Congressman J. C. Watts, a former football player, said that he has always been guided by some very good advice: "My father taught me that you are responsible for your choices, good or bad, and you have to live with them, not blame anyone else."

We all know that Harry Truman had a sign on his desk in the Oval Office that said, "The buck stops here." Unfortunately, though, human beings have a long history of passing the buck. It comes easily to us. Way back in the Garden of Eden, Adam refused to accept responsibility for his own actions, telling God it was Eve who had caused him to eat the forbidden fruit. In fact Adam tried to put the blame on God, saying he ate the fruit because of "the woman you gave me." In other words, "Don't look at me, God. If you had left well enough alone, this never would have happened."

Whenever I think of someone who refused to take responsibility for his actions, my mind turns to Richard Nixon, who was driven from office by the Watergate scandal two years after winning reelection in a landslide. Even as he left office, Nixon was still refusing to take even the slightest blame for the Watergate break-in or the cover-up that followed it. There's no way of knowing for certain, but I believe that if he had stepped forward earlier in the process and taken responsibility, Watergate would have blown over, the country would have been spared much turmoil, and Nixon would have been able to finish his term. You just can't make it to the top of a mountain by blaming others for your shortcomings or leaning on others instead of using your own strength.

The great business leader Mary Crowley gives us these ten excellent words to live by: "If it is to be, it is up to me."

When a reporter for the *Indianapolis Star* asked historian Barbara Tuchman what the world would need most in the twenty-first century, she replied, "Probably, personal responsibility." She went on to explain that she meant, "Taking responsibility for your behavior, your expenditures, and your actions, and not supposing society must forgive you because it's not your fault."

During the Civil War, General Jeb Stuart signed his letters to Robert E. Lee, "Yours to count on." I like that. We all should strive to be people others can count on.

6. Perseverance

Obviously, perseverance is an important trait for anyone who wants to get to the top of a mountain.

Rich DeVos, Orlando Magic chairman, said to me once, "If I had some idea of a finish line, don't you think I would have crossed it years ago?"

Unfortunately some people give up at the very moment when they are on the verge of success. Consider this: Water boils at 212 degrees, unleashing all the power of steam. At 211 degrees, water is just moving quietly in the pot. One degree makes all the difference in the world.

When someone asked radio commentator Paul Harvey the secret of his success, he said, "I get up when I fall down."

Anthony Greenwald, psychologist at Ohio State University, said his research has led him to believe that, "In most cases in this world, all you need to do to succeed is to just keep on trying."

Reggie Jackson was known as "Mr. October" during his baseball career because he always seemed to come through in a big way during the World Series. Jackson came through most of the rest of the time too, finishing his career with 568 home runs. And yet, Jackson says, "I struck out 2,500 times in my career. Strung together, that's five years. For five years, I never touched the ball!"

People who persevere understand that success doesn't come with every swing of the bat. They know that if they keep on swinging, success will come often enough. And so Reggie Jackson, despite all those strikeouts, finds himself in the Baseball Hall of Fame.

Olympic Gold Medal–winning skier Bonnie St. John Doane said recently in an interview, "People fall down. Winners get up. Gold Medal winners get up the fastest."

▲

If I fell down, I was determined to get up. If I fell down again, I would get up again. And I was going to keep moving until I fell down and could not stand or I walked into that camp, or I walked off the face of the mountain.

Beck Weathers

▼

220

Mary Kay Ash, founder of Mary Kay Cosmetics, said, "The only difference between successful people and unsuccessful people is extraordinary determination." Someone else remarked, "The difference between being ordinary and extraordinary is that little extra."

Franklin Delano Roosevelt advised, "When you get to the end of your rope, tie a knot and hang on."

In August 2000 Dr. Jay Strack, motivational speaker and author, addressed our annual staff retreat. He closed his hour-long talk with this fascinating story: "The highest peak in the French Alps is located on the French side right along the border of France and Switzerland. When mountain climbers are attempting to reach the summit, they have an opportunity to stop and rest halfway up the mountain at the Mediocre Inn (in French this word means halfway and in English it translates to the word *mediocre*).

▲

A great man is always willing to be little.

RALPH WALDO EMERSON

▼

"At this inn, climbers can stop and rest, stock up on supplies, or take refuge from storms. The climbers are wet, cold, and exhausted and start peeling off their boots and socks, heavy equipment, and clothing. There's a fire roaring in the fireplace, hot goulash and cocoa are served, and there's a place to grab a nap.

"Eighty percent of the climbers never leave the inn to complete the climb. They say to themselves, *You know, I've done more than most people or I've got a pulled leg muscle or the view here is great.*

"After a while, a handful of people get up and start putting on their equipment and then head into the cold to complete the push to the summit. It is then that some of those who stayed behind begin to get restless. They start fidgeting and pacing and some lean over the rail and look upward. They watch with envy as their friends are completing the task they set out to do.

"That's what being mediocre does to you. It leaves you with the feeling of being the best of the worst and the worst of the best. In fact maybe the most unflattering word in the English language to describe anyone or any endeavor is *mediocre*."

Whatever you do, don't quit. Don't give up. Success may be closer than you think! But you'll never get there if you give up now!

7. Humility

I've had the privilege of meeting hundreds of people the world would consider important. And something I have found to be true over and over again is that the biggest names are very often the nicest, most humble people. They are down-to-earth, seemingly unaffected by their own success. There are exceptions, of course. But the exceptions are usually the ones who are enjoying their fifteen minutes of fame. They don't have any staying power and they don't remain at the summit of the mountain for very long.

Most of those who have proven again and again that they belong at the top are humble. They thank God for the skills and opportunities he has given them. Celebrities understand their dependence on their fans and the others who help make their success possible. They take their jobs seriously, but not themselves.

They are like comedian Jerry Seinfeld, who considers his enormous success to be like expensive perfume: "I can smell it, but I'm not buying it," he said.

Now, keep in mind that humility is not low self-esteem. It's not lack of pride in a job well done. What I'm talking about is being kind to others, understanding that they are important too, taking their needs into consideration, not believing that the sun rises and sets on you alone!

Sir Edmund Hillary gained international fame when he became the first climber to set foot on the summit of Mount Everest, after several others had made unsuccessful attempts to climb the world's tallest mountain. But years later, he said, "If someone wants to believe I'm a heroic figure, fine, but . . . for me . . . I did a reasonable job at the time. I didn't get carried away then, and I never have."

In Myrtle Beach, South Carolina, for a speaking engagement, I asked limo driver Ron Joy who he would consider to be his most memorable passenger. His quick choice was Muhammad Ali: "Ali is a special person. He sat up in the front seat with me. He had time for everyone. Never turned down anyone for an autograph; just a very kind, considerate man."

I saw that in person in February 2000 when Ali and his wife, Lonnie, were honored at a banquet in Orlando. They sat at the head table, and I approached Lonnie timidly and asked if her husband

222

would sign a couple of pictures. She replied, "He'd love to. Just ask him." Ali could not have been more gracious as he signed his autograph for me—and for the hundreds of other attendees who followed my lead.

Millard Fuller, president of Habitat for Humanity, an organization that builds homes for poor families, says some celebrities show up to pound a ceremonial nail or two. Of course, he's happy to have their support. But with former President Jimmy Carter, "It's no photo op. When the last nail is being driven on Friday afternoon, he's still at work. The knowledge of what he's doing just permeates our work sites. How can somebody 50 years old say, 'I can't take it,' when a 74-year-old ex-president is out there holding the boards and driving the nails?"

Speaking of nails, football player Todd Blackledge hit one on the head when he said, ". . . one of the most important qualities of many really successful people is humility. If you have a degree of humility about you, you have the ability to take advice, to be teachable. A humble person never stops learning."

▲

Children have never been very good at listening to their elders, but they have never failed to imitate them.

JAMES BALDWIN

▼

8. Influence

Who's watching you? You might be surprised. Mary Lou Retton was eight years old when she saw Nadia Comaneci win a gold medal in the 1976 Olympics. "I can remember looking up at my mother and saying, 'Mommy, I'm gonna be just like her one day.'" Was this just a little girl's dream that would fade with time? No. That desire stayed with her, and eight years later, Mary Lou Retton brought home Olympic gold of her own.

At the end of his long, magnificent career with the Philadelphia Phillies, Mike Schmidt said, "I hope I have touched kids in a positive way. To me, everyone who wears a uniform carries the responsibility of becoming a positive role model. When I think about it, that is more important than any home run, any play, or any statistic."

How I wish more of today's athletes and celebrities believed that. Instead, we get comments like, "I'm paid to play the game, not be a role model." Well, every time you put on a uniform or every time you get up there on that stage, you are a role model, whether or not you want to be one.

But you don't have to put on a uniform or play a guitar to be a role model. The truth is that everyone is a role model for someone! And that means that all of us need to be on guard to ensure that our actions are exactly what we want them to be. As philosopher Edwin Hubbel Chapin said, "Every action of our lives touches on some chord that will vibrate in eternity."

▲

One man, with courage, makes a majority.

Robert F. Kennedy

▼

Author John Maxwell says that the average person directly or indirectly influences ten thousand other people during his or her lifetime, and those who are in leadership positions influence many, many more. "That's the reason leadership carries such an incredible responsibility . . . namely, that of making certain you're heading in the right direction; that the decisions you make are character-based and the route you choose is a good one."

Albert Schweitzer said, "Example is not the main thing in influencing others. It is the only thing." Of course, influence cuts both ways. As Oswald Chambers writes, "If we keep ourselves long enough under the right influences, slowly and surely we shall find that we can form habits that will develop us along the line of those influences."

That's why it's important to go out of your way to stay in the presence of extraordinary people.

9. Courage

It takes courage to climb a mountain, but courage is not the absence of fear. Courage is continuing on in spite of your fear. Courage is getting out of bed at one in the morning and heading out into the cold and snow when you'd really rather be someplace where it's warm and comfortable. As Eddie Rickenbacker said, "Courage is doing what you're afraid to do. There can be no courage unless you're scared."

The only way to develop most of the character traits we've discussed in this chapter is to begin putting them into practice. This is also true of courage. The only way to develop courage is to act courageously. Writer Cora May Harris said, "The bravest thing you can do, when you are not brave, is to profess courage and act accordingly." As I was climbing up the mountain I kept thinking about John Wayne who said, "Courage is being scared to death, but saddling up anyway."

Martin Luther King said, "On some positions, cowardice asks the question, 'Is it expedient?' Then expedience comes along and asks the question, 'Is it polite?' Vanity asks the question, 'Is it popular?' Conscience asks the question, 'Is it right?' There comes a time when one must take a position that is neither safe, nor polite, nor popular . . . but one must take it, because it is right."

Sometimes, on a mountain, it takes courage to keep going. Other times, it takes courage to back down and let the mountain win, knowing that you can come back again another day. As Winston Churchill said, "Courage is what it takes to stand up and speak; courage is also what it takes to sit down and listen."

During the reign of Alexander the Great, a young man was guilty of cowardice during a fierce battle. He was brought before the great king, who demanded to know his name.

"Al . . . Al . . . Alexander, sir," came the reply.

Alexander the Great angrily grabbed the young man by his shoulders and shook him. "Either change your behavior," he shouted, "or change your name."

Look at your life. What do you see? Are you lacking in courage, or in any of the other attributes we've discussed in this chapter? If so, there is time to change your behavior. There is time to replace doubt with faith, dishonesty with integrity, laziness with hard work, immaturity with maturity, and irresponsible behavior with responsibility. If you see that you have a tendency to give up easily, you can change and become someone who perseveres in the face of difficulty, you can exchange arrogance for godly humility, you can become a person of positive influence, and you can exchange cowardice for courage.

If you work hard to develop all of these nine character traits, I know success will be yours! See you at the top of the mountain!

Epilogue

Never measure the height of a mountain until you have reached
the top. Then you will see how low it was.

DAG HAMMARSKJÖLD

It has been almost five years since I first set foot on Mount
Rainier. And yet I still think about that mountain every day. It
remains an important part of my life, and always will be, even if I
never see it again. But I hope that doesn't happen. After all, the
mountain defeated me the first time I tried to climb it. Now I owe
it one!

Nonetheless, I am grateful to the mountain for what it taught
me—for giving me the lessons contained in this book. I am also
grateful to you for taking this journey with me. I hope that what
I've shared with you will help you be a better climber, able to overcome every mountain life puts in your path.

On my weekly radio show, I have the pleasure of talking to many
wonderful people who are in the sports business. Recently, I had
a delightful talk with John Steadman, who's been covering sports
for Baltimore newspapers since 1948.

He told me that one of his most memorable interviews came
shortly after he became a reporter. The subject of the interview

was Frank "Home Run" Baker, a star from the early days of base-ball, who was then seventy-seven years old and recovering from a stroke at his home in Trappe, Maryland.

Steadman remembered how they sat in Baker's living room on a late autumn afternoon with the sun coming through the half-closed venetian blinds, painting a herringbone pattern on the floor. He recalled that Baker was warm, gentle, and had "the biggest hands I've ever seen."

Near the end of their conversation, Frank Baker said something John Steadman will never forget: "I hope I never do anything to hurt baseball."

Here was an elderly man, recovering from a stroke, who still wanted to be certain that he behaved honorably in everything he did, that he never did anything to tarnish the game he loved.

My closing prayer—for you and for me—is that as we are climb-ing the mountains God sets before us, we too will act carefully and honorably every step of the way—that we will never do anything to bring the slightest dishonor to God or his kingdom.

Now, before we say good-bye, let's go back over the Ten Life Lessons learned from Mount Rainier:

> **Life Lesson Number Ten: Live large.** Every day do something that scares you. Each accomplishment will build your con-fidence to take on even bigger challenges.
>
> **Life Lesson Number Nine: Learn patience.** Ice is slippery. So is life. It has always been true that "slow and steady wins the race." Slow and steady will also get you to the top of the mountain.
>
> **Life Lesson Number Eight: Adapt to changing conditions.** On a mountain, conditions can change dramatically from one moment to the next, so stay focused and be prepared to change your approach when the situation calls for it.
>
> **Life Lesson Number Seven: Control what you can control and forget the rest.** If you spend your time taking care of what you *can* control, the things you *can't* control will almost always fall in line.

Life Lesson Number Six: Join the team. Success in life is not only made possible by a team effort but takes on its deepest meaning within the unity and community of the team.

Life Lesson Number Five: Follow the leader. What is it that you want to accomplish in life? Someone who is experienced and competent in that area, and who is willing to lead by serving, can be of invaluable help in getting you there.

Life Lesson Number Four: Give up the right to complain. Complaining will not keep you warm when it's cold, nor will it get you a single inch closer to the mountain's summit. You may be surprised at how much more you're able to accomplish when you maintain a positive attitude.

Life Lesson Number Three: Don't get careless. Enjoy the mountaintop experiences in life. But most mountaineering accidents happen on the descent, not the ascent, so stay focused. As Muhammad Ali said, "It isn't the mountains to climb that wear you out; it's the pebble in your shoe." Take care of the little things and you'll be just fine!

Life Lesson Number Two: Have fun! If you have a difficult time telling the difference between work and play, you're well on your way to personal success.

Life Lesson Number One: Concentrate on character. Character counts everywhere in life, especially on a mountain.

I sincerely hope that as you seek to live out these lessons from the mountain, you will find that the words of Isaiah 33:16 will come true for you: "This is the man who will dwell on the heights, whose refuge will be the mountain fortress."

Until we meet again—onward and upward!

BIBLIOGRAPHY

Ali, Hana. *More than a Hero*. New York: Pocket Books, 2000.

Allison, Stacy. *Beyond the Limits*. Wilsonville, Ore.: Book Partners, 1999.

————. *Many Mountains to Climb*. Wilsonville, Ore.: Book Partners, 1999.

Amatt, John. *Straight to the Top and Beyond*. Canmore, Alberta, Canada: Kan-Sport Publishing, 1995.

Anker, Conrad, and David Roberts. *The Lost Explorer*. New York: Simon and Schuster, 1999.

Bass, Dick, and Frank Wells. *Seven Summits*. New York: Warner Books, 1986.

Beckey, Fred. *Mount McKinley*. Seattle: Mountaineers, 1993.

Bell, Steve. *Seven Summits: The Quest to Reach the Highest Point on Every Continent*. Boston: Bulfinch, 2000.

Bonington, Chris. *Heroic Climbs*. Seattle: Mountaineers, 1994.

————. *High Achiever*. Seattle: Mountaineers, 1999.

Boukreev, Anatoli. *The Climb*. New York: St. Martin's Press, 1997.

Breashears, David. *High Exposure*. New York: Simon and Schuster, 1999.

Breashears, David, and Audrey Salkeld. *Last Climb*. Washington, D.C.: National Geographic Society, 1999.

Buhl, Hermann. *Nanga Parbat Pilgrimage*. Seattle: Mountaineers, 1998.

Burfoot, Amby. *The Runner's Guide to the Meaning of Life*. New York: St. Martin's Press, 2000.

Burgess, Adrian and Alan. *The Burgess Book of Lies*. Seattle: Mountaineers, 1994.

Child, Greg. *Mixed Emotions*. Seattle: Mountaineers, 1997.

———. *Postcards from the Ledge*. Seattle: Mountaineers, 1998.

———. *Thin Air*. Seattle: Mountaineers, 1998.

Chisholm, Margo. *To the Summit*. New York: Avon, 1998.

Cinnamon, Jerry. *The Complete Climber's Handbook*. Camden, Me.: Ragged Mountain Press, 1994.

Clark, Jamie, and Alan Hobson. *The Power of Passion*. Calgary, Alberta, Canada: Inner Everests, Inc., 1997.

Clifford, Hal. *The Falling Season*. Seattle: Mountaineers, 1998.

Coburn, Broughton. *Everest—Mountain without Mercy*. Washington, D.C.: National Geographic Society, 1997.

Coombs, Colby. *Denali's West Buttress*. Seattle: Mountaineers, 1997.

Couillard, Mike and Mary. *Miracle on the Mountain*. New York: Avon, 1998.

Crane, Nicholas. *Distant Mountains*. New York: Random House, 1998.

Curran, Jim. *High Achiever: The Life and Climbs of Chris Bonington*. Seattle: Mountaineers, 1999.

———. *K-2—Triumph and Tragedy*. Seattle: Mountaineers, 1987.

Dickinson, Matt. *The Other Side of Everest*. New York: Three Rivers Press, 1997.

Firstbrook, Peter. *Lost on Everest: The Search for Mallory and Irvine*. Lincoln-wood, Ill.: Contemporary Books, 1999.

Fyffe, Alan, and Peter Iain. *The Handbook of Climbing*. New York: Penguin, 1990.

Gammelgaard, Lene. *Climbing High*. Seattle: Seal Press, 1999.

Gillman, Peter, and Leni Gillman. *The Wildest Dream: The Biography of George Mallory*. Seattle: Mountaineers, 2000.

Graydon, Don. *Mountaineering: The Freedom of the Hills*. Seattle: Mountaineers, 1992.

Greig, Andrew. *Summit Fever*. Seattle: Mountaineers, 1985.

Haberl, Jim. *Dreams and Reality*. Vancouver, B.C.: Raincoast Books, 1994.

———. *Risking Adventure*. Vancouver: Raincoast Books, 1997.

Haston, Dougal. *10 High Places*. Seattle: Mountaineers, 1972.

Hattingh, Garth. *The Climber's Handbook*. Mechanicsburg, Pa.: Stackpole Books, 1998.

———. *Climbing the World's Best Sites*. New York: Rizzoli, 1999.

Hemmleb, Jochen. *Ghosts of Everest*. Seattle: Mountaineers, 1999.

Herzog, Maurice. *Annapurna*. New York: Lyons Press, 1997.

Hillary, Sir Edmund. *View from the Summit*. New York: Pocket Books, 1999.

Hobson, Alan. *From Everest to Enlightenment*. Calgary, Alberta, Canada: Inner Everests, Inc., 1999.

———. *One Step Beyond*. Canmore, Alberta, Canada: One Step Beyond Publishing, 1997.

Holzel, Tom, and Audrey Salkeld. *The Mystery of Mallory and Irvine*. Seattle: Mountaineers, 1999.

Hornbein, Thomas F. *Everest—The West Ridge*. Seattle: Mountaineers, 1980.

Houston, Charles. *Going Higher*. Seattle: Mountaineers, 1998.

Houston, Charles S., and Robert H. Bates. *Five Miles High*. Helena, Mont.: The Lyons Press, 1939.

———. *K2: The Savage Mountain*, rev. ed. North Salem, N.Y.: Adventure Library, 1994.

Howe, Nicholas. *Not without Peril*. Boston: Appalachian Mountain Club Books, 2000.

Jackson, Monica, and Elizabeth Stark. *Tents in the Clouds*. Seattle: Seal Press, 1956.

Jenkins, McKay. *The White Death*. New York: Random House, 2000.

Jones, Chris. *Climbing in North America*. Seattle: Mountaineers, 1997.

Kauffman, Andrew J., and William L. Putnam. *K2—The 1939 Tragedy*. Seattle: Mountaineers, 1998.

Kocour, Ruth Anne. *Facing the Extreme*. New York: St. Martin's Press, 1998.

Krakauer, Jon. *Eiger Dreams*. New York: Doubleday, 1990.

———. *Into Thin Air*. New York: Villard, 1997.

Kropp, Göran, *Ultimate High—My Everest Journey*. New York: Discovery Books, 1997.

Leamer, Lawrence. *Ascent*. New York: William Morrow, 1982.

Long, John. *Close Calls*. Helena, Mont.: Falcon, 1999.

———. *The High Lonesome*. Helena, Mont.: Falcon, 1999.

———. *Sport Climbing*. Evergreen, Colo.: Chockstone Press, 1997.

McGovern, Mike, and Susan Shelly. *The Quotable Athlete*. New York: McGraw-Hill, 2000.

Mantovani, Roberto. *Everest*. Seattle: Mountaineers, 1997.

Mason, Marilyn. *Seven Mountains*. New York: Plume, 1998.

Messner, Reinhold. *All Fourteen Eight-Thousanders*. Seattle: Mountaineers, 1999.

———. *The Crystal Horizon*. Seattle: Mountaineers, 1989.

————. *Everest —Expedition to the Ultimate*. Seattle: Mountaineers, 1999.

————. *Free Spirit: A Climber's Life*. Seattle: Mountaineers, 1998.

————. *My Quest for the Yeti*. New York: St. Martin's Press, 2000.

————. *To the Top of the World*. Seattle: Mountaineers, 1999.

Miller, Dorcas S. *Rescue*. New York: Thunder's Mouth Press, 2000.

Molenaar, Dee. *The Challenge of Rainier*. Seattle: Mountaineers, 1971.

Monteath, Colin. *Hall and Ball—Kiwi Mountaineers*. Seattle: Mountaineers, 1997.

Morris, Jan. *Coronation Everest*. Short Hills, N.J.: Burford Books, 1958.

Muir, John. *Mountaineering Essays*. Salt Lake City: University of Utah Press, 1997.

Norman, Geoffrey. *Two for the Summit*. New York: Dutton, 2000.

O'Connel, Nicholas. *Beyond Risk*. Seattle: Mountaineers, 1993.

Olsen, Jack. *The Climb up to Hell*. New York: St. Martin's Griffin, 1998.

Perrin, Jim. *Mirrors in the Cliffs*. Birmingham, Ala.: Menasha Ridge Press, 1983.

Poindexter, Joseph. *To the Summit*. New York: Black Dog and Leventhal Publishers, 1998.

Potterfield, Peter. *In the Zone*. Seattle: Mountaineers, 1996.

Powers, Phil. *Wilderness Mountaineering*. Mechanicsburg, Pa.: Stackpole Books, 1993.

Rebuffat, Gaston. *Starlight and Storm*. New York: Modern Library, 1999.

Reuther, David. *The Armchair Mountaineer*. Birmingham, Ala.: Menasha Ridge Press, 1989.

Ridgeway, Rick. *The Last Step*. Seattle: Mountaineers, 1980.

Ringholz, Raye C. *On Belay!* Seattle: Mountaineers, 1997.

Rose, David, and Ed Douglas. *Regions of the Heart*. Washington, D.C.: National Geographic Society, 2000.

Roskelley, John. *Stories Off the Wall*. Seattle: Mountaineers, 1993.

Salkeld, Audrey. *World Mountaineering*. Boston: Little, Brown, 1998.

Scott, Doug. *Himalayan Climber*. San Francisco: Sierra Club Books, 1992.

Sherman, John. *Sherman Exposed*. Seattle: Mountaineers, 1999.

Simpson, Joe. *Dark Shadows Falling*. Seattle: Mountaineers, 1997.

————. *Storms of Silence*. Seattle: Mountaineers, 1996.

————. *This Game of Ghosts*. Seattle: Mountaineers, 1998.

————. *Touching the Void*. New York: Harper and Row, 1998.

Steck, Allen. *Ascent*. Golden, Colo.: American Alpine Club Press, 1999.

Steele, Peter. *Eric Shipton—Everest and Beyond*. Seattle: Mountaineers, 1998.

Tibbaalls, Geoff. *Everest*. Italy: Carlton Books, 1998.

Todhunter, Andrew. *Fall of the Phantom Lord*. New York: Anchor Books, 1998.

Unsworth, Walt. *Everest*. Seattle: Mountaineers, 2000.

Waterman, Jonathan. *In the Shadow of Denali*. New York: The Lyons Press, 1998.

———. *The Quotable Climber*. New York: The Lyons Press, 1998.

Weathers, Beck. *Left for Dead: My Journey Home from Everest*. New York: Villard Books, 2000.

Whittaker, Jim. *A Life on the Edge*. Seattle: Mountaineers, 1999.

Whittaker, Lou. *Lou Whittaker: Memoirs of a Mountain Guide*. Seattle: Mountaineers, 1994.

Wickwire, Jim. *Addicted to Danger*. New York: Pocket Books, 1998.

Willis, Clint. *Climb*. New York: Thunder's Mouth Press, 2000.

———. *Epic*. New York: Thunder's Mouth Press, 1997.

———. *High*. New York: Balliett and Fitzgerald, 1999.

Wilson, Ken. *The Games Climbers Play*. Birmingham, Ala.: Baton Wicks, 1996.

Pat Williams is senior vice president of the Orlando Magic and is a popular motivational speaker. He helped found the Orlando Magic in 1987 and then guide it, as general manager, from an expansion club to one of the top teams in the NBA in just a few short years.

Before taking the helm in Orlando, Williams was general manager of the Philadelphia 76ers for twelve years, including its 1983 championship season. He was also general manager of the Atlanta Hawks and the Chicago Bulls.

Pat is one of the country's top motivational and inspirational public speakers. He has written nineteen books, including his version of the birth of the Orlando Magic, *Making Magic*, and his autobiography, *Ahead of the Game*.

Pat and his wife, Ruth, live in Florida and are the parents of nineteen children, fourteen of whom are adopted.

If you would like to contact Pat Williams directly, please call him on his direct line at (407) 916-2404 or e-mail him at pwilliams@rdvsports.com. Mail can be sent to the following address:

Pat Williams
c/o RDV Sports
8701 Maitland Summit Boulevard
Orlando, FL 32810

If you would like to contact Pat Williams regarding speaking engagements, please contact his assistant, Melinda Ethington. She may be reached at the above address or on her direct number at (407) 916-2454. Requests can also be faxed to (407) 916-2986 or e-mailed to methington@rdvsports.com.

We would love to hear from you. Please send your comments about this book to Pat Williams at the above address or in care of our publisher at the address below. Thank you.

Twila Bennett
Revell Publishing
6030 East Fulton
Ada, MI 49301
http://www.bakerbooks.com